THE MILFORD SERIES

Popular Writers of Today

VOLUME NINETEEN

The Clockwork UNIVERSE

of
Anthony Burgess

by Richard Mathews

R. REGINALD

THE Borgo Press

SAN BERNARDINO, CALIFORNIA

MCMLXXVIII

To Julie

Library of Congress Cataloging in Publication Data:

Mathews, Richard, 1944-
    The clockwork universe of Anthony Burgess.

        (The Milford Series: Popular writers of today; v. 19)
        Bibliography: pp.
        1. Burgess, Anthony, 1917-   —Criticism and interpreta-
tion. I. Title.
PR6052.U638Z79   823'.9'14   78-14552
ISBN 0-89370-127-0 (cloth); ISBN 0-89370-227-7 (paper)
ISSN 0163-2469

Produced, designed, and published by R. Reginald, The Borgo
Press, P.O. Box 2845, San Bernardino, CA 92406. Composition
by Mary A. Burgess. Cover design by Judy Cloyd.

First Edition———December, 1978

PREFACE

Anthony Burgess may very well be the greatest living English novelist. His range of subject, his erudition, his blend of intimate sensitivity and intelligent wit, and his skill with the sounds and nuances of language are all qualities which mark him for distinction. In twenty-three years of professional writing he has created an impressive body of work, an *oeuvre* including more than twenty excellent novels and a distinguished array of non-fiction. With nearly a quarter-century of writing behind him he has shown himself to be both more flexible and more brilliant than many of his more highly-touted contemporaries among American authors. For one thing, most of the writers on this side of the Atlantic have been nationalistic and regional in focus. This has served to heighten their anecdotal strength and personal fervor, but it has also narrowed both their vision and their themes. Burgess is international in sensibility and universal in thematic concern. In his stories he conveys the weight of global time in three dimensions—past, present, future—each commanding accute human responsibility.

This study traces some of the thematic and temporal concerns which led Burgess to write his apocalyptic, futuristic works, including *A Clockwork Orange*, a book which fulfills a natural thematic development from his earliest fiction. Yet even as he completed his dystopian timepiece he had begun creating another group of novels (including much of his best writing) determined less by clockwork time—external demands and mechanical definitions—than by the tempo of the human heart and mind—the inner timeless impulses to love and to create.

The metaphor of the clockwork universe provides a useful touchstone for considering the ten novels briefly examined here, and it is a motif extended and developed throughout his work; but Burgess has already beaten clock time as he has transcended national borders through fiction which constantly breaks beyond imposed and conventional thinking. He refers to his books as "serious entertainment" and sees himself as "a sort of professional man of letters, making a living out of words." He has made a living and a reputation which require more than this quick introductory glimpse to elucidate. There are more than enough novels beyond the conventional face of the clock to fill another Milford Series study, and Burgess is still writing.

A fine craftsman and a literary innovator, Burgess has already permanently influenced the style and form of the modern English novel. His sense of challenge and responsibility remains undiminished: "I wish I could live easier; I wish I didn't have the sense of responsibility to the arts. More than anything I wish I didn't have the prospect of having to write certain novels, which must be written because nobody else will write them." While he manages to maintain an image of himself as "a provincial boy scared of being too nattily dressed," he has clearly joined the ranks of our modern literary greats, and can be favorably compared to authors like Thomas Mann, James

Joyce, William Faulkner, Aldous Huxley, Samuel Beckett and Vladimir Nabokov.

Burgess doesn't "think that the job of literature is to teach us how to behave," but he does "think it can make clearer the whole business of moral choice by showing what the nature of life's problems is." In other words, he must first define the clockwork enemy; once we see the situation clearly, then perhaps it can be controlled. For Burgess personally and artistically this definition begins with the global holocaust of World War II, which redefined racial, political, individual, spiritual, and temporal values for the modern world.

A different metaphor will be necessary for the sequel to this introductory study, an image for the novels in which clocks do not click steadily, compelling man to march through their obscure, inexorable cadences to violence and to death; a different metaphor where time instead hangs dependent upon individuals, folds unpredictably at the edges of experience, and wrinkles across the unique contours of a single frail existence. One possibility is the visual metaphor created by Salvador Dali in 1931: "The Persistence of Memory." In that human time enshrined by memory, time is permanently molded to creative vision; the vanity of clockwork time is partially redeemed as it is in Ecclesiastes: "Wherefore I perceive that there is nothing better than that a man should rejoice in his own works; for that is his portion." Burgess has practiced this advice of the preacher in his own book *Re Joyce*; there will be time to apply it to the remainder of the Burgess *oeuvre* as well. For now, we can rejoice more fully in the clockwork universe if we recall that in a later book, a different time, Burgess has young John Keats experience an epiphany as he affirms, "I am something altogether apart from this machine," and has the poet Enderby prophesy: "this very moment, this very word will be Eden. . . ."

1. *A VISION OF BATTLEMENTS*

Burgess's first novel, *A Vision of Battlements*, was written in 1949 but not published until 1966, at a time when he was personally distant from the youthful innocence and despair which it depicts. When he wrote it, Burgess was 32, just barely detached from his protagonist, a young man in his late twenties caught up in wartime action. In his introduction, Burgess himself establishes the autobiographical context for his fiction, observing that this novel was written only three years after he had left Gibraltar (the novel's setting). Like his hero Richard Ennis, Burgess served there in the second half of his six years war duty, "as a sergeant and subsequently as sergeant-major." Burgess was a training lecturer in speech and drama; his hero Ennis does similar duty tutoring music and sermonizing the life drama of politics (idealistic socialism with a tinge of revolutionary zeal). *Battlements* not only examines World War II milieu, but also attempts to draw the battle lines in a new war, a fight for individual identity after the collective nightmare of a world where ordinary politics, art and love are unknown and can be either friend or foe.

When he wrote the book Burgess says he "had no intention of setting myself up as a novelist. . . . my ambition was to be known as a composer of serious music." He had, in fact, already written several major compositions, but found himself at the time "empty of music but itching to create." *Battlements* is a rich literary orchestration of serious personal themes set forth in a style which is musically and metrically informed. The fact that it depicts Ennis as a struggling composer, haunted by melodies, yet unable to fully realize his conceptions ("Concepcion" is his lover), makes this book a fascinating starting point for becoming acquainted with Burgess and some of his recurring themes and rhythms.

The introduction is actually full of contradictions; Burgess first says he wrote the book "to see if I could clear my head of the dead weight of Gibraltar. I had lived with it so long that it still lay in my skull, a chronic migraine." Then, having suggested these autobiographical aspects, he backs off just a little: "I had better say at once that the personal pain has little to do with the content of the story. No character is based on any real person living in Gibraltar at the end of World War Two. The names and personalities and events have more to do with Virgil's *Aeneid* than with remembered actuality. 'Ennis,' who tries to blue-print a Utopia in his lectures and create actual cities in his music, is close to 'Aeneas,' 'Agate' to 'Achates,' 'Turner' to 'Turnus.' Lavinia is Lavinia, Barasi is Iarbas, his name anagramatised. Concepcion is Dido, a dark-skinned widow loved and abandoned." Burgess deepens the fiction by moving continually along three planes— the personal, the historical, and the mythical—and though three types of temporal dimension are utilized, it is interesting to note that they linger on the past and present, with the future uncertain and indecipherable. Many mythological types appear and develop in his fiction, figures which suggest enduring ancient principles, and some of the characters Burgess invents in this book appear mythically in other writing. Ennis is featured prominently in *The Worm and the Ring*, and serves as a point of reference in *The Long Day Wanes*. Like the Roman poet Virgil in the *Aeneid*, Burgess is fully conscious of writing in the shadow of a towering classical tradition. He patterns his hero after Aeneas, with full awareness that his great predecessor James Joyce had already worked greater wonders with the Greek classical epic in his new *Ulysses*. Aeneas is patently a less original hero than Ulysses or Achilles, a secondary type of epic figure molded and weighed down by literary predecessors, almost as though the character himself were dimly conscious of the chaotic and degraded state of affairs in the present.

Virgil wrote his *Aeneid* after the Roman emperor Augustus had ended the civil wars which wrecked the bankrupt Roman empire following the assassination of Caesar. Virgil intended his poem to become the great national epic, with a hero to represent "the race destined to hold the world beneath its rule." Burgess wrote in the declining years of another race which had felt called upon to rule the world; in fact, the growth and expansion of the German empire during the Second World War offer yet another foil to the British imperium. The great war established new political boundaries, and accelerated the gradual crumbling world control of Great Britain. As a hero, Ennis is inclined to accelerate rather than reverse the process.

On the purely literary level these parallels are embodied in the constant authorial awareness of the shadow of great literary giants from the "golden" age of the novel—or in Virgil's case, from the ideal models of classical Greece. Burgess acknowledges his own humility as a writer of the "modern" period he chronicles in *The Novel Now*. He explains: "We must not, then, look for giants in the period we are going to study." It's a simple fact of life that "novelists nowadays do not care sufficiently or believe enough. Masterpieces spring out of conviction." Rome (like England in Burgess's day) had started to lose faith when Virgil wrote, and his superhero Aeneas does not ultimately succeed through an overstated heroism in recreating the essential fabric of classical conviction which was then unravelling. Aeneas lacks the cleverness of Odysseus, and the driving, purposeful rage of Achilles; he goes through the motions of epic hero for seven years in Virgil's attempt to connect the great Greek past to the shakey Roman present, and thereby prepare a greater future. Yet Aeneas dies short of his goal to found Rome, and the final connection to that city is through the "Julian" line (Iulus, the sun of Aeneas and Creusa), which established Roman hegemony through Julius Caesar to Augustus. Ennis, too, stops short of his goal; he fails to establish a new life on Gibraltar and finally is shown trying to return to his old home, which no longer really exists. He has no son to complete his failed quest. His name and his actions suggest *ends* rather than beginnings; and as his name implies, Ennis is *in us* all.

Julian Agate, Burgess's equivalent of Achates, is Ennis's closest friend and mentor. His first name ironically suggests that he, not Ennis, may be related to the patrician Caesar line. His second name is indicative of his complex functions as an alternative to the barren sterility of Gibraltar rock— agate is composed of layers, often concentric, in trap rock, and can be intimately-joined varieties of silica, chalcedony, carnelian, amethyst, quartz, jasper, opal, and flint. Agate is much used as a polished ornamental stone, and Julian in this novel carries level after level of importance, as much in terms of structure as of character. Halfway through the book, for instance, in a casual remark, he introduces a theme which haunts this novel and the remainder of the Burgess *oeuvre*. He is the first character to present the metaphor: "You must write me a ballet, you really must," he tells Ennis. "Something bright and *clockwork*, hard clean lines, like Satie." The multi-layered Julian is both the dancer and the dance, and in his off-hand remark he presents not only the problematical clockwork metaphor, but its ultimate solution, the containing and transforming of it through controlled artistic vision. Nonetheless, in the novels through *A Clockwork Orange* each Burgess protagonist finds himself unable to compose to clockwork; we are asked to consider the problem, and whatever solution we can find will be merely in us.

The precision and regularity of the timing implicit in this request for a clockwork composition are completely missing in Ennis's life—he is wandering, unpunctual, uncertain, governed by apparent oracles and omens like Aeneas, driven by a mechanism larger than himself. Julian, on the other hand, is neat and puntual, precise in his habits and his dance. They form a pair of almost Manichean opposites whose differing propositions are thematically detailed in all the early novels. As a writer, Burgess again conforms to his own advice in *The Novel Now*: "We shall be more inclined to assess the stature of a novelist by his ability to create what the French call an *oeuvre*, to present fragments of an individual vision in book after book, to build, if not a *War and Peace* or *Ulysses*, at least a shelf."

In the prologue to *Battlements*, Ennis is being transferred to Gibraltar, where he is to serve the remainder of the war as a teacher attached to the Army Vocational and Cultural Corps; ironically, he is supposed to be pre-aring men for useful lives after the war ends. The first sentence is nearly incomprehensible: " 'A. V. C. C.' said the big blonde Wren." It could be a line from a fairy tale about birds or from a nonsense book. The explanation is actually simple. Ennis has stuck up a conversation with girl from the Woman's Royal Navy Service (WREN) who is reading initals from Ennis's shoulder patch. Wartime dislocation and confusion, and a more general difficulty of conveying meaning through the very designations intended for communication are conveyed immediately in this puzzling exchange of linguistic guesswork.

"I don't think I've ever seen them letters before," the blonde says. Of course, she has literally seen the letters, but here, in this circumstance, they have no meaning to her, or to the reader, for that matter. Ennis remarks that "The Army calls these numerals," and the Wren sees past his words to a kind of truth: "Then the Army's daft. . . . Numerals is numbers. Letters is what these are. Come on, tell us what they mean." The colloquial and slightly ungrammatical Wren is a marked contrast to Ennis, who teases her by replying in Latin: "Arma Virumque Cano Corps," and when she looks blank, "Army Vocational and Cultural Corps." The first page of the book exhibits wide linguistic range, including the colloquialism of the lower-class Wren, the refined English of Ennis, together with his French and Latin remarks, and the inexplicable "militarese" which surrounds them. The "A. V. C. C.", he tries to explain, is "to prepare for the future. . . . to get the men ready for when this lot's all over. To teach them how to build a new world." Efforts to rehearse a stage show (with Ennis playing piano, and the Wren reciting doggerel) are upset by heavy weather, and intruded upon by the constant introspections of Ennis. He is aware of an enemy more vast than any war: "A number of faces had coalesced into a single image—the destroyer, the anti-builder, a Proteus capable of being time, the sea, the state, war, or all at once. It wanted cities down, love broken, music scrambled. Ennis the builder cursed and wept in the ruins."

As the ship nears the great Rock of Gibraltar, the purpose of Ennis's assignment becomes unclear, the reason for the war uncertain, the actual enemy in doubt, the course of lasting love uncharted. A Lance-Corporal declares: "Our voyage in itself is a symbol of the course that English history took," and a Sergeant remarks, "Down here on the messdeck it's still England, still Avonmouth, and hence still the past. Up there it's Africa and the future. . . . Time is really space after all." Ennis, like Aeneas or Virgil or, most personally, Burgess, knows the need for vision to help prepare for the future, his own as well as others'. A fellow shipmate, Julian Agate, is a "ballet-dancer, one-time Petrouchka praised by Stravinski and patted by Diaghilev, "witty, urbane, and homosexual. Together they face an odd Christmas Eve: "They awoke with a shock to find their future was upon them. . . . the giant threatening rock, the vast crouching granite dragon, the towering sky-high sphinx. . . . an incubus, but also their bride and mother." Time is ever-present, in the odd irrelevancy of the Christian calendar (a holiday nearly without meaning in the context of this war), in the speculations about history and myth, and in the direct awareness of past and future. Ennis, composing music in his head, finds the "winding line of his sonata lost sonority, faded to bat-squeak. . . . Like Andromeda, he thought, chained to this rockface till time shall send the deliverer, they now had to learn the great gift of patience." He faces an enemy of time-space far less specific than the Germans. The big blonde Wren waves to Ennis as she leaves for her new assignment in Cyprus, where Venus was born, and Ennis climbs aboard a truck moving "into the future that was now the present. The past lay well behind them, ... And behind that? None of them wanted to think."

It is a masterful Prologue, introducing the haunting themes of love, time, and isolation, which are more fully developed throughout the rest of the book and in Burgess's later novels as well. Time is shown through a confusing clockwork, its rhythms constantly repeating themselves like the recurring ideas and motifs of a musical composition; repeated mythological references link the present to the past, and both in turn point toward the future (also a factor in the *Aeneid*). The novel has begun *in media res*, both with respect to the war itself and Ennis's life, but the opening chapter moves the action a year forward. Ennis is making love to Concepcion, a widow living with her father, having gained entrance to her house as a guitar instructor. Ennis protests: "But I do love you," uselessly, for Concepcion has finally decided that it is sex Ennis wants not her. At the very same time that he is trying to express what he feels in words she will understand, "the musk of the dark skin, the tang of sweat in her hair, the faint residuary breath of garlic whetted a compassion in him that was near to love"; simultaneously, however, he is reviewing in his mind a letter from his wife Laurel which heralds a separation. The past (his relationship with his wife) and future (their separation, his wife's marriage to someone else) are in constant counterpoint to his present affair with Concepcion. And these in turn are in conflicting temporal relationship with Ennis's duties. "When he looked at his watch the sweat started again and his head (the musical direction *martelato* came unbidden)hammered. He should now be lecturing. . . Prisoners assembled prompt at twelve-thirty in the little fortress twenty minutes' climb away. Twelve-forty by his watch." He fumbles for excuses. "Could he pretend to have been taken suddenly ill? No, there was the business of having to report sick. His watch, that was it, his watch had stopped." Clockwork pervades the book, but it is not progressive time. The excuse Ennis manufactures is, in a sense, true. His time *has* stopped with respect to any ordinary, incremental, developmental sense. He practices patience and repetition, at odds with a world that moves to a different cadence; temporal changes wash around him without touching his inner reality. Concepcion finds she is pregnant by Ennis, but she decides to marry Barasi, an old persistent, wealthy, pudgy suitor. Laurel meanwhile seems to have a change of heart, and sends Ennis a note urging him to get himself promoted, to move up the ranks and make something of himself and find a permanent position on Gibraltar so she can join him when the war is over. But Ennis is too far out of touch to follow through on any of this.

His sole preoccupation and his only comfort is composing music. He turns out a dirge-like wedding piece for Concepcion, and throughout the novel struggles with a Passacaglia and Fugue. In fact, the passacaglia sets the form for the book—a slow, dignified dance which originated in Spain, it expresses very well the warm and Romantic side of life in Gibraltar, in marked contrast to the stiff English administration which holds the natives in check, and which is represented by the Army officers who are at once unbendingly disciplinary and morally decadent. The musical form is based around an ostinato figure, a recurring melodic form, composed with variations over a constantly repeating ground base. Ennis describes the sounds which haunt his mind's ear: "It had formed itself out of the 'C C C' of Concepcion and the 'B flat AA E flat' of Barassi. . . . a tune that would hold together the most fantastically divergent variations."

The fictive and narrative structure which Burgess utilizes in the novel is, in effect, a verbal elaboration of the Passacaglia. The echoing motifs from the *Aeneid* imply a kinship in theme and variations, all played against the recurring bass line of history and of myth. The fact that the Passacaglia is first performed at the wedding of Ennis's lover (the woman who bears his child) to another man adds a considerable ironic and grotesquely comic angle. Burgess always verges on comedy, though the atmosphere rarely becomes light enough for outright laughter. It is laughter held in check by the pressure of circumstances too dangerous for comedy.

Battlements plays out a chain of repeated thematic motifs, including the inability fully to love, or to understand what love means, the inability to compose or conceive (figuratively or literally) without this basic emotion, the overwhelming pressure of time as it determines and influences behavior, the alternative memory of time as it becomes history or myth, and finally, the fact which throws all of these thematic problems into sharpest focus, the ultimate end of time in personal terms—death. Death haunts the edges of this novel—as it does all of Burgess's fiction. It is the certain confrontation that will put an end to all of our excuses about love, and cause us finally to know both *eros* and *thanatos*; it is the final measure of definition leading to history, myth, or oblivion.

The time element is nearly overwhelming in the early account of Barasi's wedding. Concepcion, while bearing Ennis's child, is to be married on "the anniversary of the death of Ennis's father, and the end of the war in Europe." To Ennis it seems "a day of corpses: the disfigured remains of his father, the cadavers that lay for the slow work of sorting and interment all over filthy Europe, the lost body of Concepcion. He could hardly think of her as alive, rather as a Persephone doomed to enter the house of Dis, laid out for the final enormity, a necrophilic nightmare." The appalling juxtaposition of love and death is not shrugged off by the fact that we believe Barasi to be something of a fool, or that we recognize Ennis to be in many ways an uncertain adolescent. He has been, after all, involved in war from about the age of twenty, with no normal opportunity to develop or mature. When Ennis seeks his own identiy, it is wrapped up in the panorama of death which surrounds him: "Ennis was thrust back into remembering what he was here for. On August 5th Hiroshima was blasted, with over seventy-eight thousand dead." There follows a marvelously-written parenthesis, another curious manifestation of *orange*: "(They were to see it later in the hot cinema, pungent with the smell of orange peel, full of the healthy sweat of white-decked sailors, the huge mounting stalk blossoming into white-hot smoke at its crown, spreading and spreading, a ghastly flower; they were to hear the unctious booming of the soundtrack: the sun's energy tamed to an essentially peaceful end. They that live by the sword shall perish in freak light-storms, weird mock-photography, cerements of parched oven-stinking skin, delayed-action diseases, the proliferation in dark silent tracts of unearthly cancers.)"

Hiroshima was the ultimate vision of battle which pierced the eyes and consciousness of the modern world. It was a vision overwhelming to Burgess, one which he dare not let his readers forget. Not only did it suddenly throw the value of an individual life into a new and nearly meaningless perspective (when we can kill seventy-eight thousand or more with the push of a single button, the importance of the individual diminishes), it also became a symbol of collective guilt for modern man. This guilt is part of the implication of the "delayed action diseases" Burgess points out, the "unearthly cancers" which plague our lives and hasten the death, and which will finally annihilate us altogether. Burgess puts it another way in *The Novel Now*: "Kafka has influenced us all, not merely writers. When he first read *The Trial* aloud to his friends, their response was laughter. Nobody laughs now. We have all come to feel a powerful and desperate guilt since the revelations of Belsen and the blasting of Hiroshima: there are few of us now, Christian or not, who would reject the doctrine of Original Sin. And, with the breakdown of society as our fathers knew it, the creation instead of huge conurbations where everybody is lonely, the Kafka theme of man's essential isolation strikes us poignantly. He was a pilot of the pain of contemporary man."

Ennis, like Burgess, is a "lapsed Catholic," and the shadow of Original Sin, like the shadow of God (which is never clear, and is often mistaken for the shadow of authority [particularly in the Army] or the shadow of death) casts shades of meaning across the book's action. Burgess said in his *Paris Review* interview with John Cullinan in 1971-72 that "The ideal reader of my novels is a lapsed Catholic and failed musician, short-sighted, color-blind, auditorialy biased, who has read the books that I have read. He should also be about my age." This, of course, seems to be a rather specialized audience, and when Cullinan asked Burgess if he thought this might have kept his novels "from becoming better known in England and America," the author admitted, "The novels I've written are really medieval Catholic in their thinking, and people don't want that today." This is not to suggest that the moral structure Burgess reaches toward in *Battlements* and other fiction is merely traditional Catholic theology. On the contrary, he has insisted, "I'm entitled to an eclectic theology as novelist, if not as a human being"; but Original Sin and its concommitant guilt are clearly part of the difficulties Ennis faces as a hero, part of the general problem of eternity and meaning Burgess never shrinks from addressing. It is not an abstract, philosophical investigation, but an intense, intimate, personal daily struggle.

As he explains in the same interview, "We really absorbed hell—perhaps a very Nordic notion—and think about it when committing adultery. I'm so Puritanical that I can't describe a kiss without blushing." Ennis shares a similar embarrassment early in the novel when he is called to Major Muir's office, and confronted with his real reason for giving "guitar lessons" to Concepcion. Muir seems to possess omnipotent knowledge in this interview, and as the novel develops, he becomes increasingly God-like, even on the explicit level. Muir tells Ennis that he knows all about this clandestine romance: "I know every single little thing that there is to be known about that, Ennis. You watch your step. Because if there's going to be any trouble, Ennis, by God, I'll make you wish you were never born." One critic has pointed out that R. Ennis is a reverse anagram for "sinner"—a man haunted by sin and threatened by a secular God figure in Major Muir.

A. A. De Vitis in his Twayne book, *Anthony Burgess*, (1972), has provided the best general introduction to date. DeVitis links Burgess's lapsed Catholicism with fictional elements of black comedy as it presents an essentially Manichean view of life: the doctrine, regarded as heresy by the Catholic church, that life is a constant conflict between light and dark, spirit and matter, with matter being seen as dark and evil. The Manichean system, composed as it is of Gnostic Christianity, Buddhism, Zoroastrianism and various other elements, is a fascinating background for the internationalism Burgess deals with, entirely appropriate in a situation where one is trying to pick up the pieces of a world view.

De Vitis did not invent this idea; in the same *Paris Review* interview, Burgess was asked specifically: "Several years ago you wrote, 'I believe the wrong God is temporarily ruling the world and that the true God has gone under,' and added that the novelist's vocation predisposes him to this Manichaean view. Do you still believe this?" In *Battlements* Muir is a prime example of this "wrong God" who has usurped control. It is not therefore unusual that Burgess responded to his interviewer affirmatively: "Novels are about conflicts. The novelist's world is one of essential oppositions of character, aspiration, and so on. I'm only a Manichee in the widest sense of believing that duality is the ultimate reality."

Stranded by Concepcion's decision to marry Barasi, Ennis turns to his wife Laurel and tries to establish a more secure position on Gibraltar so she can join him there. But, although he summons all his courage to approach Muir, his overtures are ridiculed and denied. Drunk and maudlin, Ennis determines to visit Concepcion. On his way to see her he falls from the boat and is completely immersed—a sort of ritualistic baptism. De Vitis sees this as the beginning of a descent to the underworld—which it is in a sense, since Julian Agate (Ennis's later roommate) is something of a decadent;

but it is also, like the best temporary visits to hell, a cleansing and sobering ceremony rather than an experience of eternal punishment. Ennis finally sees his roommate Bayley as the slob he is, and reforms his own life by moving in with Julian. Julian keeps the quarters spotless and tidy, does fine embroidery in his spare time, and mothers Ennis during his crises. He even manages to get Ennis to keep appointments. Ennis is able to resume serious composing, and the themes of his composition weave memory and desire for Concepcion into the Passacaglia form, despite a symbolic baptism and "a changed life, a fresh beginning." Speaking about her to Julian, Ennis is suddenly taken "again and again and again down the score, the whole orchestra hammering out the theme in unison." He is startled to realize that "I speak of her as though she's dead." Julian replies: "In a sense she is," but like haunting repetitions of theme in the Passacaglia itself, the unrealizable Concepcion from which Ennis has been forcefully separated is as dead as the still-born orchestral score on which he labors.

His period of sharing rooms with Julian coincides with a growth in his creative work. Scheduled to conduct an evening of his own music, he even manages to recruit a symphony, reheasing regularly; but the Army suddenly intervenes. Ennis is arbitrarily ordered to duty the very night of the concert, forcing its cancellation. Major Muir seems to carry some vindictive impulse against Ennis, as though he has been judged and found lacking by a jealous, vengeful god. The creative delight which Ennis briefly experiences is too good to be allowed. Ennis puzzles over the question, sensing that he may have the flaw of Achilles, a type of arrogant pride: "Was he perhaps unworthy of this, too—not the little fame, but the pentecostal bestowing of the ability to create? Had one to give something back? One gave labour, the sweating for hours over the scoring of a single bar, but perhaps there was something else, something timeless, something commensurate with the divine gift. For some reason the word *hubris* kept coming into his mind. Did the gods decide on the nature of the payment?"

The painful self-consciousness of this question spotlights the guilt of Ennis (and perhaps of Burgess)—another repercussion of the Fall into generation in the Bible. Man is condemned to labor, but will that labor bear genuine fruit? In the case of Ennis, destiny decrees no. Major Muir orders him to duty; Ennis refuses and is arrested. The concert never takes place. And Quartermain ironically observes of Major Muir: "He's turning into God. *Deus fio*. But at least the Roman emperors were humble enough to think in terms of an expanding pantheon. Also, they waited till they were dying. Christianity's done a lot of harm to types like him." Ennis knows this clearly. He earlier had told Quatermain, "In other words, he's God." But this definition is no more meaningful than the truncated initials in the book's first sentence; or the Army's decision to refer to letters of the alphabet as "numerals." Major Muir is clearly *not* God despite the arbitrary power he wields. Ennis is left with "No faith in anything, it seemed. Not even in art. There remained charity. There remained hope." But by the end of the chapter, with no reprieve forthcoming, charity too has been eliminated and only hope remains: "There was hope left, of course. There was always hope."

The unreality of Muir's action, its arbitrary and impersonal quality, push the book further into a mythological frame of reference. Major Muir is called to the War Office for a conference, but his deification continues in his absence, supervised by Captain *Apple*yard; an ideal post-lapsarian taskmaster, he confuses apples and oranges. Appleyard holds regular religious services, reminding the men that the Major "is in spirit with you, even, in a sense, watching you. He has never betrayed you—do not you betray him." Burgess in this ironic deification elaborates a question which will continue to interest him: is the wrong God ruling things? Is this a substitution of petty bureaucracy for deity? And do the people accept it? Ennis refuses to attend the services "on conscientious grounds," but most of the men are there.

The painting of murals to celebrate noteworthy accomplishments of the Major offers an opportunity for outrageous mythological overstatement. Julian "had in fact executed, in a charming rococo style, a series of small panels dealing with the loves of Zeus. The god was depicted as descending on Leda, Dadae, Europa. The face of Muir crowned the body of the swan, the huge frame of the bull, and glinted through the shower of gold. In each case the copulation was presented in frank detail, but any suggestion of the pornographic (though in the strict etymological sense the paintings were all of that) was mitigated by the pennant labels attached to the ladies: Art, Science, Technology." Appleyard has them painted over before the Major returns.

Ennis perfunctorily pursues his lecture duties; the men appreciate him for his idealism and human eccentricity. He conveys his own faith in liberty and equality and the possibility of an ideal society. He also exhibits some sympathy to the move toward an independent Gibraltar, and when his idealism fades, he is just as apt to dismiss the troops to the local bar as to belabor the fine points of political change. The final phase of Ennis's drama is played out in his encounter with a nearly surreal figure. He meets Lavinia while returning from a lecture, and looks up at the rock: "The apes were soothing to watch. Their pattern of life was simple, their language and gestures unambiguous, their inhibitions few." Lavinia is practically a double for his wife, and even seems to share some of Laurel's conversational habits. She writes poetry and agrees reluctantly to show it to Ennis. Faintly romantic, alienated, frightened, her work interests Ennis; but he is predictably more interested in her physically. She is reluctant to yield, but Ennis lures her to his room, shows her one of her poems he has set to music for soprano and strings, and she gives in. Their love-making ends in dialogue, however; Lavinia seems to read him clearly: "You want God, and yet you want to be alone. You obviously worship your wife, and yet you say you hate her. . . . And then there's the question of your art. You call it your art, anyway. I would say that it's more of a hobby," and she repeats Coneybeare's belief that "You just have no ear. . . It's just something you don't happen to be born with." By the end of the chapter, Lavinia teases him, "How about telling me you love me?" and he can only rage, "Ah, to hell with love."

The surreal encounter with his wife's double is amplified by a series of uncanny revelations and accidents which conclude the book. An antagonist presents himself in the form of Turner, the new physical training officer, a handsome, aggressive, obnoxious, overbearing sort. He tries to beat up Ennis, but Ennis accidentally kills him in the struggle. Asked to select several poems to be read at an assembly, Ennis picks several highly sensual selections from Garcia Lorca and Saint John of the Cross, but it turns out that the assembly is of schoolchildren, and his performance causes a great scandal. He receives a letter that his wife declaring at last that she is leaving him and going to America. Finally, he is ironically promoted, a clear indication that there is no corelation between reality and the arbitrary exercise of power, and then transferred home.

Before leaving, however, he agrees to visit a fortune teller with Julian. Mrs. Carraway looks at the Tarot—a man hanging upside down from a tree, a tower struck by lightning, a bloody moon. "Things have not been going well" she tells him. "Things will not go any better." Ennis and Julian leave for Spain to check on Barasi and Concepcion and to enjoy one last fling. Howling below her window, he learns that Concepcion is dead, and sees that he has made a fool of himself. "I must learn to grow up," he says. "I can't put it off much longer." Time is asserting its reality beyond anything else, and Concepcion's death is the most absolute reminder that it is irrevocable.

The novel is a panorama of great conflicts unresolved, the yearning to be creative, to be free, to be loving, all of these aborted and destroyed. Authority seems invested and bestowed without reason. Surely the wrong god is in control. At the end, when his isolation in time and space is most absolute, Ennis is on board a ship returning to a past which does not exist: "When you get this I shall be gone," his wife's letter begins. Ennis can do nothing more than turn the experience into art: "Images droned through his brain without sequence as he stared steadily at the bay. From among the drift of his mind a theme emerged. With a tiny pulse of excitement he heard its possibilities. A strong quartet, obviously. Last movement. There must be another theme logically anterior to this one; that would make the first movement. No real sonata form, no great length. Economy. Absolute unity of construction. On the back of Laurel's letter he drew five rough lines and noted down what he heard." He leaves Gibraltar "looking along the ship's wake at the dwindling past. It shook impotent fists, trying to assert an old power, but it knew that it was becoming too small to be anything but ridiculous or lovable.''

The final heroic achievement in the book is this ability to glimpse a vision of the past as "ridiculous or lovable." It is a detachment born of great pain, but a vision which at least still holds some hope for human feeling and for love. It also allows in its own dwindling measure the absolute end to a charge of *hubris*; and puts into perspective the petty battlements Ennis has been forced to command. (In one of Burgess's little ironies, we are told that the main reason the British hold Gibraltar is so American insurance companies can insist that the Rock will never fall!) Still, in all this, Ennis, like many a Burgess hero, is a detached observer who finds himself in circumstances beyond his control, particularly at the mercy of societal bureaucracies. Around him and through him we see the certain deterioration of the British empire, combined with the demand of its subject peoples for freedom and independence.

2. *THE LONG DAY WANES*

The spirit of revolution is even more evident in Burgess's Malaya trilogy, *The Long Day Wanes*. As in *Battlements*, the setting and the themes of these three fine novels is derived from the author's personal experiences. Their central character, Victor Crabbe, is attached to the education service, teaching history in Malaya. Burgess himself was Colonial Education Officer in Malaya and Borneo from 1954-1959, when illness necessitated his return to England. The Malayan trilogy was written during his years of duty in the East, and reflects much of the tension and the cultural diversity he observed there.

The title used for the American publications of these three novels serves very well to suggest their temporal concern. We are present at the waning of a "day" which has been artificially long. England's rule over her extensive foreign territories seems both undemocratic and fortuitous, and Burgess reflects seriously on the theme of paternalism in national, educational, and technological affairs. Crabbe is seriously convinced he is there because he can offer these primitive people some kind of educational enlightenment, yet he is forced repeatedly to see his own actions, and those of his fellow Englishmen, as ridiculous, false, lazy, inferior, and morally decadent. How an attitude of enlightenment can be maintained before the sordid side of British dominance is one of the questions forced upon both Crabbe and the reader.

TIME FOR A TIGER

The first novel in the trilogy has a wild and wooley sound about it, as if it were going to be a jungle adventure story. But like the civilized veneer the British occupation has imposed atop the native culture, "tiger" has been reduced from its savage jungle danger to the brand name of a beer. The tale is set off by Blake's "Tiger, tiger burning bright/in the forests of the night," and the Manichean "fearful symmetry" which seems so much a part of the Burgess world view. This frightening balance is suggested in the opening inscription from Arthur Hugh Clough: "Allah is great, no doubt, and Juxtaposition his prophet." One other strong source of literary allusion resounds throughout that story: T. S. Eliot's poem, "The Love Song of J. Alfred Prufrock," full of stylistic and thematic juxtapositions. Eliot has a tiger, too, and he warns us in "Gerontion" that "The tiger springs in the new year. Us he devours." The attitude of hopelessness which permeates "Prufrock" also infuses the trilogy, and the protagonist, Victor Crabbe, may have taken his name from Eliot's persona: "I should have been a pair of ragged claws/Scuttling across the floors of silent seas."

Juxtaposition is a technique used frequently throughout the trilogy, and particularly in the first novel. An element typical of comedy, in which the contrast between high and low extremes provokes laughter, this contrast in tension is skillfully maintained to achieve an effect which has been called by some critics "Black Comedy," but which may actually be closer to a slightly detached existential or Kierkegaardian *Weltschmerz*. . . or Angst. Too much serious pain is implied. *Catch-22*, for example, is a far less *ordinary* fictional reality than Burgess describes. And the British sensibility overall—a sense of responsibility, intellect, serious moral purpose, and propriety—all these elements help to define the Burgess perspective in quite a different way from American writers offering somewhat comparable studies of the postwar period. Whatever we might call his style, Burgess does have the distinction, in *Battlements* of having written one of the first tragi-comic visions of the war. His *Long Day* trilogy develops distinctive narrative style and voice, and utilizes juxtaposition and allusion in ways similar to Eliot in "Prufrock" or "The Waste Land"—neither of which could be called Black Comedy, but both of which have comic elements.

The first and most dramatic juxtaposition in *Tiger* occurs in the opening dialog: "East? They wouldn't know the bloody East if they saw it." Contrasts between East and West pervade the book, and as in *Battlements*, there is a built-in judgement against Crabbe for befriending the natives. This stems from his desire to understand what he considers to be a fascinating culture. But the British purpose, tacitly accepted by all those in significant power positions, is to establish and promote British culture and to stamp out the primitive Malay traditions. This attitude persists contradictorily with the awareness that an independent Malaya cannot be far off. Everyone speaks of the pressure to make the native self-sufficient. They mean, in effect, that they want colonial puppets who can be trusted to carry on tradition in a safe and predictable manner maintaining the habits and values British culture has imposed.

Crabbe, like Ennis, faces deep conflicts in his personal love relationships. In a sense, Crabbe begins where Ennis has left off; Crabbe has already faced the death of his loved one (a central event of *Battlements*)—his first wife has fallen victim to a technological world. She died when her car went out of control on an icy day in January and plunged through a flimsy bridge fence to a watery death. Her presence dogs his relationship with his second wife, Fenella, whom he doesn't really know. They are forced to test their relationship to one another against their encounter with the foreign land. The Western conventions of love are set against a mixture of Eastern traditions which allow no kissing, segregate men and women from an early age, substitute the "marriage contract" for romantic love, encourage harems, etc. Crabbe seems unable to define his own situation, partly because his parameters for understanding these things have been strongly enlarged by this cultural encounter. Does it, after all, make good sense to have more than one wife?

A simple British melodrama gets played out against the Malayan backdrop. The opening is run, as it were, before the curtain, where we meet Flaherty, Nabby Adams and his smelly dog, where we grasp the strange existence of "tinned soups, tinned sausages, tinned milk, tinned cheese, tinned steak-and-kidney pudding, tinned ham. . . ." Nabby is totally dependent on alcohol, and particularly drawn to warm Tiger beer. His life is ruled by his need for beer money. With the first appearance of Crabbe we get a larger view of the scene: "The river Lanchap gives the state its name. It has its source in deep jungle, where it is a watering-place for a hundred or so little negroid people who worship thunder and can count only up to two. They share it with tigers, hamadryads, bootlacesnakes, leeches, pelandoks and the rest of the bewildering fauna of up-stream Malaya. As the Sungai Lanchap winds on, it encounters outposts of a more complex culture: Malay villages where the Koran is known, where the prophets jostle with nymphs and tree-gods in a pantheon of unimaginable variety." Malaya is a country of vivid factuality and mythic overtone, a very rich situation for the modern novelist (see the "magic realism" practiced by Gabriel Marqeuz Garcia and others). As Victor Crabbe sleeps, he is "drawn into that dark world where history melts into myth." The mythic dimension transposes historic time into another realm, and by developing the relationship between history and myth, and showing how one may be perceived as another, Burgess directs his readers to undertake the metamorphosis.

Battlements presented a hero (Ennis) who was struggling to understand his identity through a similar process: "But Ennis pushed his wife back beyond history, to myth. It was the best thing to do; it would ensure a kind of fidelity." In the trilogy Burgess exposes myths about the British way of Empire, as set against the more primitive Malay traditions, including tribal religions and even voodoo. This classic juxtaposition of old and new, East and West, is dropped against a far more complicated and mixed atmosphere than the racial stand-off in Gibraltar: "The two modern towns of Timah and Tahi Panas, made fat on tin and rubber, supporting large populations of Chinese, Malays, Indians, Urasians, Arabs, Scots, Christian Brothers, and pale English administrators. The towns echo with trishawbells, the horns of smooth, smug American cars, radios blaring sentimental pentatonic Chinese tunes, the morning hawking and spitting of the *towkays*. . . ."

The racial mixture is complemented stylistically through the broad vocabulary Burgess employs. Linguistic confusions, multi-lingual puns, and an obvious delight in the pure sounds and textures of words play significant roles in his fiction. There is even a glossary of Malayan derivatives and Anglicized native words. As the book develops, interest in translation, and the inclination of the central characters to desire communication with each other across language barriers, amplifies the importance of the linguistic motif.

The plot of this book is comic and nearly farcical in bare outline. Since his wife's accident, Crabbe has refused to drive a car; he and Fenella walk everywhere, quite literally "closer" to the Malayan people. But Fenella is homesick for England, and wants a car so she can get out to social affairs and cultural events. Nabby Adams and his sidekick Alladad Khan contrive an elaborate scheme to buy a car cheap and sell it to Crabbe for a tidy profit. Through the motor transport division of the British Army, they will provide upkeep on the car, and Alladad Khan will act as driver. Crabbe agrees, but in order to buy the car and pay for a driver, he is forced to give up the expense of maintaining his native mistress in Rahimah. The scheme appears to be beneficial for nearly all sides, since Nabby and Alladad Khan put an end to Fenella's boredom. She grows fond of them, developing both a human and mythic attachment. De Vitis observes that Nabby is "a figure of myth." His remarkable aphoristic pronouncements appeal to Fenella's bookish nature (at one point she reads to him from "The Waste Land"), "and she never ceases to be surprised by the quality of his mind and the range of his knowledge. Perhaps a Eurasian, six feet, eight inches tall, Nabby becomes for Fenella a Prometheus being pecked at by the eagles of debt and drink, a minotaur hawling helplessly in the maze of debt."

The car they sell Crabbe is called an "Abelard," another philosophically intriguing and comically interesting detail. Peter Abelard, the boldest theologian of the 12th century, struggled to resolve conflicting values between his life as a scholar and his deep love for Heloise. He married his beloved, but was spiritually drawn away from her by the overwhelming demands of his work. They were finally separated. That Crabbe should be riding, and by the end of the novel *driving* a car named after this neo-Aristotelian theologian is symbolically an index to his deepening character. The car changes the lives of each of the primary characters, but the change is unpredictable.

This automobile is the vehicle for a key journey of the novel, the trip to

Gila. Nabby must go there to inspect cars, and he suggests that the others might find it an interesting side trip. Unfortunately, the route passes through an area where an uprising for Malayan independence has spawned violent revolutionary communist activity. The trip is riddled with problems and delays; Fenella is sick and dizzy; heavy rains obscure their visibility. The vivid scene establishes both literally and metaphorically that the foreign jungles and revolutionary natives cannot be clearly discerned by the distorted English vision. Burgess describes the scenery and events in a surreal and hallucinatory style. De Vitis speaks of this climax in terms of the title: "When the party arrives within sight of the town, Fenella is sick, and the jungle locks its cage. The tiger of the novel's title has sprung. The voyage to Gila brings into prominence the religious importunities of the novel's theme, and the allusion to Blake's poem, 'The Tiger,' tentative before, suddenly becomes obvious. The inferno imagery, the suggestion that the dog Cough must, like Cerberus, be appeased, the reference to the evil snake gliding through the jungle and to a monkey making a disturbance in the trees—all the surrealistic aspects of the episode support a religious as well as a psychological interpretation, a voyage to the heart of darkness." As the tiger springs we may recall again from Eliot's "Gerontion," "In the jurescence of the year/came Christ the tiger." Is it crucifixion or salvation about to spring?

Nabby is left in Gila, but the trip back is plagued by more problems. The car breaks down and it becomes clear that Crabbe won't be able to get back for the school games he is supposed to supervise that afternoon. In a horrifying attack, the rebels shoot at the car as they approach the city outskirts. Alladad Khan is hit, and Crabbe takes the wheel: "It was quite a time before he realized that he was driving again. Driving well, moreover. And really exhilerated. He almost felt like singing." Crabbe has accomplished a spiritual breakthrough. He has apparently conquered the past and established his ability to act decisively in the present. But even while this is occurring, the future is preparing to reverse and overthrow the present. When Crabbe returns, he is called in by his director and dismissed. The boys had refused to participate in the games Crabbe was supposed to supervise, and Victor is blamed, even though he had previously tried to warn the director of a student plot. Things go better for Nabby. When he gets back from Gila he finds himself with a winning lottery ticket worth $350,000. Crabbe, who has held the stub for Nabby, has the satisfaction of showing it to his boss and pretending he has won the money. Nabby pays off his huge debts, gives enough to Crabbe and Fenella to start a school when they return to England, sees Alladad Khan promoted to Sergeant, and helps the Crabbes prepare to leave for their new school assignment.

The first book of the Malayan trilogy is resolved by the pure operation of chance. Whatever the partial breakthrough seemed to signify for Crabbe, it certainly did not establish his ability to choose and to act decisively in present time. At the end, the characters move into a future which more closely resembles the random spinning of the roulette wheel than the clockwork mechanism of the precise, neo-Artistotelian machinery of the Abelard. Even the mechanics of the fictional technique seem consciously clumsy at the end. Burgess has employed a *Deus ex Machina* for deliverance as the long days of empire wane, a slim chance only for the individual characters who find themselves inheritors of the present situation. Crabbe is, like the Abelard whose namesake automobile he finally drives, a man of conscience. The place for conscience in the present life becomes one of the major questions of the book, as it is asked politically of England and America, as it strikes to the heart of any teacher whose job it is to inculcate the wisdom of the past, and as it strikes the individual most intimately in his mind and heart.

THE ENEMY IN THE BLANKET

At the end of *Tiger*, Crabbe finds he has been "done in" by "an enemy in the blanket," one of the very students he might have counted on for support. The phrase—with overtones of internal conflict and betrayal, and even the suggestion of a connection between the hotbed of Malaya and the problem-ridden marriage bed Crabbe shares with Fenella—carries over as the title of the second book in the trilogy. *The Enemy in the Blanket* follows Crabbe even deeper into the East, into the political, cultural, and philosophical turmoil of the heated environment. The title suggests an inevitability—the cliche that "one makes his bed and then has to lie in it"—true for both the characters and the empire in the developing trilogy. Pure luck and apparent good fortune had cleared the way for a happy ending in *Tiger*: the luck of the raffle assured Nabby of a liquor supply for life; the sipping of a love potion apparently resolved Crabbe's marriage problems; and Crabbe was able to leave the shool with a moral victory over the monomaniacal headmaster (who closely resembles Ennis's commanding officer in *Battlements*). The enemy has been difficult to pinpoint in Burgess's first two novels, but in the central book of the trilogy "We have found the enemy and it is us."

Fate and an inevitability unrelieved by the fortuitous luck of *Tiger* lingers over Crabbe's arrival at his new assignment: "Where the British were sent, there they had to go. That was how they had built their Empire, an Empire now crashing about their ears." The sense of being aboard an enterprise headed for destruction lingers about his marriage as well, since Fenella has received an anonymous letter (signed merely "The Voice of the East") telling her of Crabbe's unfaithfulness. "You're disgusting. I'm going to leave you," she tells him on the third page, but her departure and the departure of the British are both reserved for the closing pages of the novel.

The Crabbes' arrival in the State of Dahaga is confused; there is no one to meet them at the airport, and they are uncertain where to go. They hire native trishaws and set out for town. Along the way they meet a car driven by a European, an old schoolmate of Crabbe's as it turns out, Rupert Hardman. Rupert is "very much a white man" since his skin is "deficient in pigment"; to make him even more conspicuous, his face, disfigured when his plane was shot down in the war, is still scarred by plastic surgery. The sins of the past, the scars of a war, are literally visible on Rupert. Hardman tells them they shouldn't be travelling with the natives because of violence and unrest in the area (another scar from the past now marked upon the present), and takes them himself to the district supervisor, Talbot. Hardman's reflections give us as much insight into Crabbe as into Hardman, since Crabbe doesn't seem to notice the scars: "Crabbe had never noticed very much, though, the world of sensory phenomena meaning less to Crabbe than the world of idea and speculation. So it had been at the University, when Hardman, in his first year, had gone to hear Crabbe talk to the Communist Group, Crabbe the well-known and brilliant, for whom everyone prophesied a First. Crabbe had had no interest in the coming revolution, no love for the proletariat, only an abstract passion for the dialectical process, which he applied skillfully to everything." The dialectic will be one of the breakdowns of the book; and this past image of Crabbe will significantly impact on events, despite the different views he has come to hold.

They arrive at Talbot's house to find a Scottish soldier from the "Home Guard" leaving the bedroom of Mrs. Talbot. A short time later (the Home Guard safely away) Talbot arrives, paunchy and pompous, a composer of bad poetry and consumer of huge meals. His wife's affair is easy to understand, but it casts a dubious light upon love in the East. The anti-romantic view of marriage is compounded by Hardman's decision to marry 'Che Normah, a wealthy widow whose two previous husbands were slain by communist bullets just before they were about to leave Maylay without her. Hardman feels trapped by life, too insecure about his appearance to try to make a go of his legal practice or teaching in England, and without the necessary resources, personal or financial, to succeed in Maylay. 'Che seems to offer him a way out, but their marriage contract specifies he must forsake his newly-embraced Catholic religion, thereby giving up his only good friend Father Laforgue, to embrace the Moslem faith. This religious stipulation establishes 'Che's governance over the spiritual sphere, while her "unpredictable passion and . . . robust sexual demands" coupled with her great wealth assure her dominance in the physical as well.

Hardman tries to comfort himself that a marriage of opposites is possible, and as he takes his farewell from Father Laforgue, his situation is comparable to that of Laforgue himself, a man who embraces the Catholic religion but whose bookshelves are lined with works by Confucius and other Chinese philosophers. Hardman tries to tell him that Catholicism and Islam have a great deal to say to one another, more even "than have orthodox and heterodox Christianity. It was a quarrel between men when all is said and done, and there was a healthy mutual respect. Both claimed Aristotle as master of them that know, and Dante put Averroes in a very mild place. What I mean is that you can't take Luther or Calvin or Wesley very seriously, and hence they don't count. But you can take Islam very seriously and you can compare wounds and swop photographs, and you can say, 'we're old enemies, and old enemies are more than new friends.' It's like bull-fighting and the moment of truth, when the toreador and the bull become one." But even in this strained, optimistic metaphor we can see marital disaster. Either the toreador *or* the bull will win, after all, and the fight will be over. There is irony in his rationalization, and in the line from *Antony and Cleopatra* which comes ringing clear to him as he thinks about his marriage: "The beds i' the East are soft." Shakespeare's play was a tragedy, and Antony and Cleopatra are hardly lovers to emulate.

Enemy forces Crabbe to come to terms with another aspect of his past. Overcoming his fear of driving in *Tiger* only exorcised a part of his marriage problem. He explains the situation to Hardman: "It was a ghastly business. A car smash. The damn thing went into a river. I got out all right. It was January, a very cold January. Then I married Fenella. I'd known her before: she was a post-graduate student when I was lecturing. I just couldn't get warm again. I used to shiver in bed. It was partly an accident my coming here—you know, answering an advertisement when I was tight—and also a kind of heliotropism, turning towards the heat. I just can't stand the cold." He must balance both his fear of water and his need for heat in order to retain Fenella, but Crabbe is unable to do either.

He has transported the fabled Abelard with them to Negeri Dahaga, where it attracts the attention of the local potentate, the *Abang*, a man of wealth, power, many wives, and many cars, who sets his eyes on both Fenella and the Abelard and has them both by the end of the novel. Crabbe is occupied with serious rivalries and problems at the school, where his assistant is hostile and scheming to take over. Unearthing some communist articles Crabbe had written for his college magazine, the assistant threatens to reveal Crabbe if he doesn't request a transfer. To make matters worse, Crabbe's Chinese cook, whom he inherited with the headmaster's house, is harboring and supporting Chinese rebels in the nearby jungle, further implicating Crabbe. As a matter of consolation, and seeking greater heat in bed, Crabbe has turned to Anne Talbot, a dangerous and loveless liaison in a small community with a penchant for gossip. Hostility toward Crabbe is leveled at the Abelard; its tires are first slashed, and then the entire car is burned in the school garage while Crabbe is making love to Anne (he is supposedly attending a headmasters' convention).

Hardman's marriage also does not work out as he has planned. He uses his wife's money to set up a law office, but she is an overbearing and jealous shrew, ruling his every move, exhausting him sexually. Even his religious beliefs and his friendship for the Catholic Laforgue must give way in her rage for possession of his soul: "He was not paying his way. His practice was not flourishing. He was a kept man. He drove back singing Blake's 'Jerusalem.' " He is led to the prophetic, Christian side of Blake, and a Blakean apocalypse of dialectical opposites is part of the book's finale. At the end, the Malayans are throwing the British out of their beds: "The whole East was awake." Crabbe has begun to see this, awakening himself when his bed at the convention is deserted by Anne Talbot. Anne takes up again with the Scottish Home Guard as a way of getting away from her boring husband and out of the East altogether. Alone, Crabbe reflects about his private life: "Perhaps there were really two kinds of marriage, both equally valid: the one that was pure inspiration, the poem come unbidden; the one that had to be built, laboriously, with pain and self-abasement, deliberate engineering, sweat and broken nails. . . . One could not spend one's life being loyal to the dead. That was romanticism of the worst sort. . . . It was time he cleared the romantic jungle in which he wanted to lurk, acknowledged that life was striving not dreaming, and planted the seeds of a viable relationship between his wife and himself."

He returns to find Talbot on the attack, having heard from Fenella that Crabbe must be carrying on with his wife. Fenella has been seeing a great deal of the *Abang*, and the only visible symbol of the "seed of a viable relationship between" her and Crabbe (and between the West and the East)—the Abelard—has been burnt so that it is "just a mass of old iron." Fenella, thinking deeply about their relationship, puts her demands in terms of time: "I want to see if you really love me. If you do love me you'll put the past out of your mind. I want you to break with the past. I want there to be only one woman in your life, and that woman to be me." By way of testing him, she has him take her swimming, but Crabbe has not been able to go in the water since his accident. He tells her he can't; but she insists that he claimed he couldn't drive either, until he was in the grip of a real emergency, overcame his fear, and handled the car. "That's not fair," he protests, "Water's elemental, it's an enemy, it's different. . . " At his protests she leaves him on the beach, swims far out, and suddenly screams for help, as though she has been caught by a treacherous current. Crabbe believes her in danger, even wades into the water, but turns back, unable to make the effort to rescue her. Fenella insists, "It's not different. You just couldn't make the effort this time. It wasn't really important enough. It doesn't matter. I'm not blaming you. But you see now that it won't work. I've known for some time now what I had to do. This was just a rather spectacular way of showing you."

Fenella returns to England, referring to their marriage as nothing more than a "waster of time." Alone, Crabbe sinks into his bed, sick and feverish. When Hardman, who has decided to end his bondage to 'Che and return to a modest teaching post in England, approaches Crabbe for a $2,000 loan to get back, he thinks Crabbe may be "off his head. Was history becoming a timeless dream for him?" He tells Hardman that his wife met an old acquaintance named Raffles at the Beirut airport—and Raffles eventually turns out to be Hardman's ticket out of the country, even though Crabbe refuses to loan him the money. "He's made his bed; he's got to lie on it," Crabbe rationalizes about his refusal, yet he is unable to move from his own bed: "Which reminds me that this bed needs making. I'd better get up." But he lay there still, hearing the clock march jauntily on to three o'clock, four o'clock, having nothing to get up for." He reaches a burning peak of delirium, at the opposite extreme from the cold he associates with the past: "They were roasting him over a slow fire, a human barbeque. . . . The word 'pyrexia' began to turn and topple like a snowball going downhill, smashing itself on a black winter tree to reveal a core of stone which meant 'fire.' " It is a feverish apocalypse. In a fiery vision, he sees himself consumed, in this case by Talbot who is merely "waiting till the Pyrex dish be drawn from the oven. In the dish was a baked crab." This surreal revelation is parallel to the surreal auto trip in *Tiger*, and nearly opposite in its isolation, immobility, and inability on Crabbe's part to *act*. Here he is not at all the heroic type who, under pressure of danger, can drive the car to safety, and even manage a victory-in-defeat in the honorary dinner for the school in *Tiger*. Instead, he is passively consumed by "the eternal basting," until deliverance comes in a sort of dialectical synthesis involving both *Tiger* and *Blanket*: "In the hot night the light was switched on. Crabbe heard the voice of an old man, happily chirping. The old man was giving him something to drink, something red-hot." It is Ah Wing and about 30 revolutionary Chinese from the jungles—the same crew Crabbe had earlier unintentionally abetted—now resolved to give themselves up. Boo Eng, a notorious ringleader, has been taught at an English school, and so is able to communicate easily with Crabbe. Crabbe has been brought out of the illness by a special Chinese remedy: "It is very powerful. It is tiger's liver stewed in brandy. It is better than all the European medicines." He can ask them the most important question on his mind as it emerges from its disoriented state: "What time is it? I've just no idea."

Crabbe becomes a hero, making newspaper headlines and as the British leave the province to the Malayans, Crabbe is temporarily promoted to Talbot's position of directory. Burgess neatly wraps up the plot with a shift to Hardman, who has finally broken free of 'Che, at least to the extent that he can express his own thoughts in his diary. Hardman and 'Che have joined a pilgrimage to Mecca, but Hardman, unknown to his wife, has arranged with the unseen Raffles to borrow a plane for his flight back to England. As he did in his reflections at Crabbe's arrival, Hardman is able to illuminate the end of the book with a detached, yet experienced perspective: "Granted that the whole problem of life is integration, who is to tell us how to integrate and what do we mean when we say a man is thoroughly integrated?

If we mean man is balanced and knows what he wants, I say he is a pipe-smoking moron with the sort of laugh that I associate with stupidity or madness. For I would say that it is death to be properly integrated, and then there is no change and one is independent of change in the world about one." The observation applies equally well to the international integration in Malaya, the cultural integration of East and West, and the male-female integration of marriage, as well as to the psychological integration which is perhaps its primary sense. It carries added weight, since in this marriage of Catholic and Moslem, of the fairest, frailest white man mutilated by Western technology in a Western war, and the dark and sensuous Moslem living off the wealth of slain Western husbands, there is involved most dramatically this question of integration. He concludes with a Blakean rendering of the destiny which seems to determine all the main events of the ending.

There is an accurate and nearly mythic sense to the clarity of vision both Crabbe and Hardman attain at the end of the novel. Crabbe's is most succinctly stated in the note he sends to the *Abang* regarding his Abelard: "It is perhaps appropriate that one of the last of the Western expatriates should bequeath to an Oriental potentate all that the West seems now to be able to offer to the East, namely a burnt-out machine." In the retelling of the tale of the Chinese capture, his final story to the Malays from his veranda, Crabbe himself becomes myth, the past transformed into eternity: "The story of the man from the far country who tried to help, the man who developed miraculous powers, killing the pirates and the bandits and diseases and teaching the final marvel of the word. And as he developed wings and an unconquerable fist and the gift of invulnerability he ceased to be man from a far country, he joined the heroes of the Malay Valhalla, he became the property of the open-mouthed tough brown men, cross-legged on the veranda, he became one of them." There is a union in this mythic realm, an integration of past, present, and future time, a transcendence of a kind. But it is, the reader knows, an exaggerated, highly ironic fiction.

BEDS IN THE EAST

As the Malayan trilogy moves toward its culmination, we are being asked to ponder a major historical and cultural event. The paradigm for *Battlements* was Virgil's epic and the founding of the Roman empire. That classical precedent lurks behind the Malayan scenario as well, but the more essential historical paradigm in this case is Shakespeare's drama and the British empire. The Elizabethan period holds great fascination for Burgess, a perceptive critic of Shakespeare and his times (see his book *Nothing Like the Sun*). Under Elizabeth England was well on the way to establishing the Empire on which "the sun never set." In *The Long Day Wanes*, we finally witness the setting sun, or as Crabbe tells Talbot, "the night in which no man can work." Even more specifically, the allusion behind the title of the final book in the trilogy is taken, as we have seen, from Shakespeare's *Antony and Cleopatra*, a work which presents themes of Empire (Roman and British), the meeting of East and West, the closeness of love and of death, the conflicting interests of State and the individual. In Shakespeare's great play, the title phrase of Burgess's book occurs as Mark Antony is expressing his thanks to Caesar for calling him away from the East. Antony explains, "The beds i' the east are soft; and thanks to you/That call'd me, timelier than my purposes, hither; For I have gain'd by it." Crabbe's actions take on added significance when considered against Antony's, for in many ways they are opposite. Crabbe does not allow himself to be called back, and his death is not so much suicide as destiny; allusions enrich Burgess's novels through literary counterpoint. Caesar's response to Antony's speech in the Shakespeare play can well serve as an introduction to the Crabbe we meet at the start of *Beds in the East*: "Since I saw you last,/There is a change upon you."

Crabbe is changed indeed; we are aware of significant temporal transformations as he examines himself in Chapter one: "Crabbe looked at himself: hair now riding back from his forehead, the beginnings of a jowl. He looked down at his paunch, pulled it in, flinched at the effort, let it out again. He thought it was perhaps better to be middle-aged, less trouble. That growing old was a matter of volition was a discovery he had only recently made, and it pleased him. It was infantile, of course, like the pleasure of controlling excretion, but transitional periods of history had always appealed to him most—Silver Ages, Hamlet phases, ['No! I am not Prince Hamlet, nor was meant to be,' says Prufrock.] when past and future were equally palpable and, opposing, could produce current. Not that he wanted action. But, of course, that was true of the phase, and that was why the phase didn't last long. Imagine a silver Age *Aenied*!" Alone and obsolete as the solitary English education officer in a hierarchy rapidly becoming exclusively Malayan, Crabbe is in a sense only the peripheral focus of this final part of the trilogy. In conversation with his British-educated Chinese friend Lim Cheng Po, Crabbe characterizes himself in the mold of English eccentric, a "crank idealist," as he puts it. Cheng Po, on the other hand, sees him in a different light: "Deriving an exquisite masochistic pleasure out of being misunderstood. Doing as much as you can for the natives. . . so that you can rub your hands over a mounting hoard of no appreciation."

While this outside opinion may not do justice to what must be counted as genuine idealism on Crabbe's part, both the masochistic aspect and the misunderstanding are centrally demonstrated in the novel. Perhaps most misunderstood are Crabbe's efforts to help a talented young Malay composer, Robert Loo. Crabbe has financed the boy's trip to Singapore to have his music performed and evaluated by professionals, but the boy seems to have absorbed the worst aspects of British detachment. He is not particularly grateful, and doesn't seem particularly concerned to hear his music once he has written it. Those around him, however, assume that Crabbe's interest in the boy must be sexual. And this is compounded by the fact that Crabbe has no lover at present.

The book is consistently more concerned with various racial types in the Eastern melting pot of Malaya than it is with Crabbe and the British perspective *per se*. It begins with a tight focus on Syed Omar as he recalls an incident he provoked at the farewell dinner for his superior Maniam. Omar, a Malayan, counters the speeches of praise with a racially directed outburst: "I warn you, especially you Malays, that you have enemies in your midst, and this Maniam is one of them. The Jaffna Tamils will try to grind you in the dirt and snatch the rice from the mouths of your wives and children." Crabbe is championing the lad's music partly because he recognizes great talent in the boy, but also because it is his desire to create a unified national identity for the emerging independent nation, to overcome racial conflicts and divisions. He sees this music as potentially and symbolically fulfilling that function. He sees it as "the first real music out of Malaya," an expression of the fact that the country has finally "thrown off the shackles of an alien culture." As he tries to persuade his Malayan successor Nik Hassan that it is appropriate to perform the boy's symphony at the independence celebration, he explains, "Here's the first bit of national culture you've ever had: not Indian, not Chinese, not Malay—Malayan, just that." A similar motive lies behind his desire to begin a series of parties: "I want to try and cultivate better inter-racial understanding. . . .I had an idea last night, in bed. Why can't we have meetings, say, once a week, to try and mix up the races a bit more?" Crabbe's bed in the East allows him the luxury of idealism still—the possibility of racial understanding—but the realities of the daylight world in Malaya fiercely negate the ideals.

Catalyst for the numerous failures of the book is Rosemary Michael, a Malay schoolteacher who at one time had lived in England, and who constantly waits for her English lover Joe to send her an engagement ring, marry her, and set her up in the refined British culture she so ardently desires. There are two very different suitors for her favors: Jalil, a rotund Turk, who constantly propositions the beautiful Rosemary to "come eat, come drink, come make jolly time"; and Vythilingam, a Hindu Veterinarian trying to resist his mother's choice of a bride with a large dowry. When Vythilingam thinks about Rosemary he recalls "a Tamil film version of *Hamlet*" (in Shakespeare's play, "Rosemary" is not conjoined to a "jolly time," but to "remembrance"). Rosemary's memories of Joe and England force her to fictionalize the present. When Joe finally sends her a little money—what he must consider a kind of pay-off to his mistress—she takes it as the money for an engagement ring, putting down savings of her own with it, and buying a suitably showy diamond. This, with her devotion to an idealized memory and her dream of inter-racial marriage, embodies a fantasy in some ways similar to Crabbe's. Her beauty is perfect, but

"The lack of flaw was a kind of deformity. It was not possible to say what racial type she exemplified: the eyes, black, were all East—houris, harems, beds scented with Biblical spices; nose and lips were pan-Mediteranean. Her body. . . was that of the Shulamite and Italian film stars. The decolletage, with its promise of round, brown, infinitely smooth, vertiginous sensual treasure, was a torment to the blood." She is happy to act as hostess at Crabbe's inter-racial meeting, because she thinks it is being held in honor of her engagement. Burgess (like Shakespeare) skillfully uses these two dreamers as foils to one another. Crabbe's beautiful dream of Robert Loo's music portending a harmonious Malaya is as mistaken as the dream of Rosemary to become a happy English bride. Both have a common weakness: the very lack of flaw in their vision consitutes a deformity.

The first major disillusionment of the book is the catastrophe at Crabbe's gathering. Just as he attempts to deliver his peroration advocating "intermarriage" and "a more liberal conception of religion," Syed Omar strides drunkenly into the party. He begins a tirade of racial slurs, and when they try to give him some black coffee to sober him up, mutters, "Don't like anything black." Vythilingam, also drunk, interrupts with echoes of odd phrases, "Dirty jobless Malay," and in the confusion, Crabbe finally offers to take Omar home: "The party, he felt, might as well be abandoned." But the conflict cannot be merely abandoned or contained: "In the scuffle that followed, nobody actually got hurt. Some of Nik Hassan's ginger ale was spilled on to Rosemary's dress, and the dress began to reek of brandy. 'Che Asma, disgusted, swept her hand across a row of spirit bottles, and two of these rolled over the floor, and Syed Omar tripped and fell over a bottle of rum, grasping, as he fell, at the nearest stable object, which was Mrs. Foo's right leg. The whole business was quite deplorable."

It is a marvelous comic scene, but serves simultaneously to chasten wishful idealism. The primary connections between races are violent and accidental. The dark side continues to be mixed with comedy in the simultaneous scene played opposite the party. Syed Hassan and his friends perpetuate a string of insults on Maniam. With handkerchiefs over their faces they enter his room and rob him. It is a bungled burglary, full of comic touches, including the ridiculous figure of Maniam as his sarong unwinds down to his ankles: "black bound buttocks were disclosed, short hairless legs, Maniam's shame." Tripping, he hits his nose on the door-knob, though he later claims the boys beat him. Syed Hassan is caught, bringing further shame on Syed Omar, who had already lost his job. Cultural maturity in civilized English terms seems constantly thwarted and irrelevant amid the childish bickerings nd elemental passions of the natives.

Robert Loo is subjected to a more insidious cultural bombardment. The first assault occurs when his father brings a loud jukebox into his cafe. Robert, who used to compose while working is now subjected to an endless stream of popular records. He loses his inspiration and his imagination, and his visions are trivialized. Concommitantly, his father destroys the first pages of his symphony, beginning the ultimate destruction of the promise symbolized there. When Rosemary finds that her dream of marriage with Joe is illusory (he sends her a letter explaining he's getting married, and adding: "I know when we are in bed together I shall often think of you and the things we did"), Robert Loo discovers her alone when he comes looking for Crabbe in the apartment, and makes clumsy love to her, further trivializing his desires. Loo, who symbolically embodies Crabbe's hope of a harmonious independent future, and Rosemary (remembrance), who incarnates Crabbe's dreams of perfect beauty and an imaginary romantic British past, collide to nullify one another in an inconsequential moment of present time. After their encounter, associated in his mind with *Antony and Cleopatra*, " 'He ploughed her, and she cropp'd.' ", he reflects that "the remembered noises of the juke-box did not seem so terrible."

Crabbe is asked to investigate the murder of a headmaster in a jungle school. (It is this trip which takes him away from his apartment and allows Robert Loo and Rosemary to get together so briefly.) De Vitis cogently points out that the trip "becomes within the symbolical framework of the novel a recapitulation of the diverse themes that were touched upon, expanded, but left incomplete in the previous volumes of the trilogy. On the train that takes him on the first stage of his journey to the mouth of the river where the estate is located, Victor finds in a magazine a poem written by his wife, Fenella. . . . Next he encounters Tommy Jones, who sells Malay beer; Jones of course reminds Victor of Nabby Adams [the famous beer drinker of *Tiger*] and of the trip to Gila, after which he had found himself able to drive again and temporarily close to Fenella. But the understanding achieved by the trip had proved meaningful only for a brief time, he remembers. In Dahaga, Victor had later become involved with Anne Talbot, Fenella had left him, and again an attempt to bring an understanding of the ways of the West to the East had failed."

Crabbe allows Tommy to take him along a short detour, an evening of diversion which leads him to his closest sexual adventure of the book. After plenty of food and drink, they are given women: "Crabbe's girl's name was Chin Chin, a name frivolous in sound but meaning 'Truth.' Led by the hand of Truth, he followed Tommy—in full song under the moon—down the empty street." But Crabbe tells her, when they are alone, "Thank you, but no," and nothing happens. Crabbe falls asleep, conscious of a destiny, "something unseen, unknown" leading him forward: "He had a dim notion that he ought to be keeping his body pure for this event hidden in the near future."

Destiny continues to move unseen but strong the next day. Crabbe is pondering how he will get on to his destination when Moneypenny, an Assistant Protector of Aborigines based in Mawas (where Crabbe is headed) stops his Land-Rover in town and offers Crabbe a lift. Crabbe and Moneypenny don't particularly hit it off, but Crabbe has somewhat more in common with an American sharing Moneypenny's quarters.

Temple Haynes is the only significant American in the trilogy, and serves important symbolic and historical functions. America is clearly shown (through Haynes) as the successor to the British sense of Empire; Americans are taking over with their money, scientific language, and technology. Haynes has met Fenella, and liked her poetry, and Crabbe is a bit put off at this; in fact, Haynes's whole image is antithetical to Crabbe's. Crabbe seems unable to live in the present, obsessed with history as he tries to build it into art or myth concerned for a future he feels responsible for shaping at each moment. Haynes is in touch with the moment, at least technologically: "Temple Haynes smiled indulgently and looked at his wrist-watch—waterproof, self-winding, with the date and the current lunar phase." Yet this man is also called "temple," and it is in his presence that Crabbe enjoys his most religious experience. They drive together to see a native shadow play at a village off the beaten path; the incident recalls the conclusion of *Battlements* with its fortune telling, and the prophecy of Mr. Raj in *Tiger*: "The country will absorb you and you will cease to be Victor Crabbe. You will less and less find it possible to do the work for which you were sent here. You will lose function and identity. You will be swallowed up and become another kind of eccentric. . . .You will be ruined."

The shadow play, which begins a climactic series of revelations for Crabbe, takes place in intense heat, reminding us of the fever scene in *Enemy*. They have entered the backstage *attap* hut, following the custom of removing their shoes before entering. There they see the master who will conduct the show, and the "gods demons, the comic intermediaries between the supernatural and sublunary worlds—the manipulation of which was his priest-like office." The master and the whole performance remind us of religious purpose, but the shadows are mere illusions of a master puppeteer, and backstage Temple gasps and cries out, "But the master, cool, brown, entranced, now utters the word 'Om,' identifying himself for the instance with God himself." Temple is overpowered by the heat, and Crabbe takes him outside. As he is putting on his shoes, Crabbe feels a sharp pain; he has been stung by a small scorpion, exclaiming: "My foot's on fire." The process of immobilization or crippling is nearly complete; the earlier promise evidenced in his driving the car (taking control of the course of his life) negated. His foot, like his Abelard, is being burnt. He tries to continue his journey, but the trip becomes increasingly more uncanny. Temple gives him a walking stick, helps him onto a launch, and they continue up river. On board the boat Crabbe discovers Vythilingam, hiding out from his mother and the woman she has chosen for him to marry.

He is lulled into reflection, and tries to distract himself from the pain in his foot by thinking about its opposite: " '*Hulu*,' thought Crabbe, trying to grasp at anything to take his mind off his foot. '*Hulu*,' the head. Head of my stick, Head of the river. . . . head of a religion.'' He is preoccupied with a vague religious feeling, but ''There was nothing to believe in except the jungle,'' symbol of conflict, instinct, inter-racial warfare. ''That was home, that was reality. Crabbe gazed in a kind of horror mixed with peace at the endless vista of soaring trunks, lianas, garish flowers. They were chugging towards the *hulu*, the head or fount of everything, where there was no pretence or deception.'' In this frame of mind he sees something timeless in the jungle's presence, and tells Temple and Vythlingam: '' 'History,' said Crabbe, battering his pain with words at random. 'The best thing to do is to put all that in books and forget about it. A book is a kind of lavatory. We've got to throw up the past, otherwise we can't live in the present. The past has got to be killed.' But in saying that, off his guard with the pain in his foot, he reverted to his own past, and pronounced the very word in the Northern style, the style of his childhood.'' Past and future seem to be closing in on Crabbe. He has been unable to kill off his past; unable to build a Malayan future he dreams of. He approaches the head of the river, where the two temporal realities will converge: ''The two halves of the jungle joined up and became one, and there was no mistaking one thing for another. The jungle called 'OM,' like the Malay showman of the shadow-play, one and indivisible, ultimate numen.''

At the landing, Crabbe goes ashore and meets Costard, replacement for the murdered official whose death had prompted the trip. Costard represents all the negative aspects of past Empire: ''The feudal tradition, the enlightened patriarchal principle. You people have been throwing it all away, educating them to revolt against us.'' Clockwork becomes conspicuous in this scene, with a serving boy punctually delivering fresh beers every twenty minutes. The timing is so precise that the host observes, '' 'That boy of mine's a walking clock.' He examined his watch narrowly. 'One minute to go. Time.' Sure enough. The Tamil boy smugly reappeared, bearing another large bottle.'' The boy also times his reappearances perfectly enough to keep the record player loaded with discs, and suddenly Crabbe hears a unique recording of his first wife's voice. Costard admits they were lovers, that she had planned to leave with him. Costard tells Crabbe he didn't deserve her, and orders him out of the house, yelling at him, ''You don't know what love means!. . . Your type never do!''

Crabbe moves clumsily away from the house on his bandaged foot. Vythlingam, who is waiting outside, sees only ''a white man coming'' and hides. Crabbe steps off the dock and misses the boat, falling helplessly into the river. His friend Vythlingam watches ''With only the mildest interest,'' and reflects ''Human lives were not his professional concern'' as the water settles quietly over Crabbe's body. As Prufrock says at the end of his lovesong: ''We have lingered in the chambers of the sea,/By seagirls wreathed with seaweed red and brown/Till human voices wake us, and we drown.'' Crabbe causes scarcely a ripple on the Malay conscience.

The book closes with the coming technological impact from America made clear, and the implication that it will obliterate the real possibility of a Malayan culture the way the jukebox negates Loo's native sensibilities. On the final pages, Rosemary, at a dance with a new boyfriend, trivializes Crabbe's conclusion when her fifth mouthful of Crab mousse pricks a memory: "Tears began to smudge her mascara. 'Poor Victor,' she said to an empty space by the white-clothed table, 'poor, poor Victor.'

" 'He came, he saw, he conquered,' said a quite handsome subaltern. 'Victor ludorum.'

" 'Poor Victor.' And then somebody asked her to dance."

It is Hamlet's "Poor Yorick," and Caesar's "Poor Antony" and an ironic ending for a Roman ideal of empire and heroism. De Vitis points out that his jungle setting employs symbols and allusions similar to those in T. S. Eliot's *The Waste Land* and the *Four Quartets* to comment on the contemporary cultural reality beyond the setting of this novel. He notes especially that: "The death-by-water theme, most dominant, brings into focus the trilogy's religious importunities, which are perhaps Burgess's chief concern." His final view of Crabbe is a sensitive perception of his effect on Burgess's monumental work: "For Burgess, like many before him, gives emphasis to the theory that all art is religious. Man's responsibility to his fellow man is what defines his humanity and perhaps determines his salvation. There is also a strong implication in the trilogy that the only morality left in the world is to be discovered in art. Victor Crabbe is, therefore, a character of infinite appeal. His name suggests a victory, the [crab] apple, the scavenger. And the scapegoat theme, handled tenderly, emerges through him as one of the most stunning aspects of the novel. Aristotelian peripety, underscoring his attempts to accomplish the impossible, makes Crabbe infinitely appealing and emphasizes an all-but-heroic stature." The trilogy is one of the great works of English twentieth century literature, full of warmth, humor, literacy, charm, and characters with stature and distinction. It exorcises many of the naive idealistic preachments of Ennis in *Battlements* and puts them to the test of struggle. In the end Victor's death fulfills the recognition he himself achieved: "The past has got to be killed." Burgess's first novels seem to have served something of the same purpose in his own life. They were a way of facing up to the present, to racial conflict with no easy solution, to indifference, sterility, a lack of heroism; a way for the idealist to assimilate the Waste Land by battling it out in the jungle.

3. THE DOCTOR IS SICK

Ready or not, Malaya got its independence in 1957 and Burgess moved to Brunei, Borneo, as English Language Specialist with the education department. In slightly over two years there he continued to work in the midst of conflicts and problems similar to those he had delineated in *The Malayan*

Trilogy: racial prejudices and stereotypes running head-on against human relations, vested business and political interests exercising power at the expense of real freedom or independence, and genuine love seeming to have no chance to flower in the boiling kettle of empire. Though his inclinations toward educational panaceas seemed blunted, his artist's sensibilities sharpened, and he managed to write two novels in his short time there: *The Right to an Answer* and *Devil of a State*. But in 1959 he began experiencing odd mental aberrations which could not be attributed to tropical heat. The symptoms of serious illness soon were unmistakable. He was given leave to return to England, and there doctors diagnosed a brain tumor, giving him just a year to live.

Burgess describes a scene in *The Doctor is Sick* which sounds temptingly like what must have happened in Borneo: "A lecturer on linguistics in a college in Burma who had one day, quite without warning, fallen on the lecture-room floor while lecturing on linguistics. He had been talking about folk etymology (*penthouse, primrose, Jerusalem artichoke*) and then, quite suddenly, he had passed out. He came to to find concerned, flat, delicate-brown Burmese faces looking down on him, himself saying: 'It's really a question of assimilating the unknown to the known, you see, refusing to admit that a foreign word is really foreign.' While he lay on the cool floor he could see quite clearly. . . one or two students taking down his words in their notebooks. . . . The doctors had taken a serious view of the matter, giving him a very dull series of medical examinations. A lumbar puncture had shown a great excess of protein in the cerebrospinal fluid. Dr. Wall had said: 'That shows there's something there that shouldn't be there. We'd better send you back to England to see a neurologist.' " The hero, Edwin Spindrift, is adrift in a sea of forces beyond his control, completely at the mercy of authority, robbed of his independence, helpless in a hospital bed. Though he has left the outskirts of the empire where prescriptive British education exports its way of life to the backward native peoples, Spindrift himself becomes the tiny native territory to be brought under the prescriptive British wing.

Spindrift is no better off in his wife than in his mental faculties. Sheila is leading quite an independent existence, showing up irregularly for visiting hours and often accompanied by strange new men. Charlie, one of the first of these, has a unique outlook on reality. He has never heard of linguistics, adding hurriedly, "Mind you, I'm not saying there's no such thing." as if he has suddenly recalled that Edwin has something wrong with his brain. But Charlie, it turns out, has a reasonably clear perspective; he is the first character in the book to make explicit one of its key issues: " 'Your brain's your own property,' " he tells Edwin, " 'and you don't want them fiddling about with it. Catch them trying to see inside my brain,' he said with scorn. 'Very delicate piece of machinery the brain is, not unlike a watch or a clock.' " The final territory of the brain seems to be the single hold-out against the tyrannies of empire—the mind's association with the delicacy of a watch or clock strengthens a thematic line leading to *Clockwork Orange*, and suggests that it is the only free and individual outpost in a confusing temporal continuum. In a deft piece of literary craftsmanship, it is Charlie the window cleaner, whose profession it is to remove the blur from those portals which allow us to see outside the edifices we build, who offers this clear bit of insight and advice so early in the book.

Though he is back in England, Spindrift is constantly confronted by the international perspectives established in the earlier books. In an apparently rather ordinary English hospital we meet a Negro orderly, an Indian sister with a moustache and sideboards, a Nigerian nurse, a Slav nurse, and a ward full of patients who "wore white turbans like Mecca pilgrims," "a ward full of sick hajis." The empire has come home to roost. Spindrift hasn't escaped the personal and social demands for equality, freedom, and the desperate individual search for the meaning of the word "love." All his etymological and linguistic analysis brings him no closer to a firm definition, and he is helplessly confined to bed while his wife takes up with one man after another.

Burgess has mastered a broad comic style in this novel, with more intellectual and slapstick humor than in the earlier works. To be sure, the bleak and serious edge is there, but a greater playfulness with language, more room for outrageous and absurdly exaggerated elements (which can occur freely in the patient's hallucinating state), and a happier use of irony throughout the book make this novel more completely comic. We might guess from the internal rhyme of the name "Edwin Spindrift" that he will "win" despite some "spin" and, in fact, not only does he win a contest for bald-headed men, but he more significantly wins the right to his own mind, the final independence from doctors, the establishment, and the marriage contract. His mind comes clear as though a miracle has come to pass, and the professorial doctor is cured while those diagnosing him are finally seen to be sick, like the society which produced them. The transmutation of values leans toward paradox, as suggested in the title. Edwin's delicate clockwork brain remains his own. Burgess, like Spindrift under his death sentence, may have held an attitude similar to that of his main character at the end of the book: "He felt well, rested, cured, sickened by the thought of so much sickness snoring around him. The night sister was reading in her improvised tent of bed screens; a thin beam from a lamp threw a moving golden guinea on her page. The worn silver tosheroon in the sky glowed over a city richer than the sun. The city and the land and all the world were there waiting, full of ripe fruit for the picking. He would not stay here a minute longer. . . . He would organise things differently this time." Spindrift at the end is "a gentleman with upright carriage and twirling stick, checking his wristwatch by the vestibule clock, finding the vestibule clock five minutes slow, sighing, just come off duty." Sure of his final destination, Spindrift's life is his own at last: "He was off to find Mr. Thanatos, who might, of course, be anywhere. There was no hurry, of course. Plenty of time for plenty of piquant adventures. And then Mr. Thanatos, vine-leaf-Thanatos—God of Wealth, ruler of the underworld, the Greed word for death, a terrible, not an evil god. This is the "Death Instinct" which pervades all of Burgess's writing. It neatly recapitulates the dialectical Manicheism of the Spiritual themes, and echoes a fundamental concept in Freudian psychology. Freud, examining what looked to be an inevitable periodicity—what Nietzsche spoke of as the "eternal recurrence of the same"—traced recurrence and repetition to the desire to restore a previous state of affairs. The ultimate prior state is that of non-existence, the state prior to conception, or what must be the ultimate aim of life—death. This *Death Instinct* is opposed by the desire to conceive, to create new life, involving for humans the sexual drives which Freud came to call *Life Instincts* or Eros. In the Manichean drama of Burgess's fiction, Eros and Thanatos are in shaky balance, with the artistic impulse being clearly neither one nor the other. The desire to create, in literature, music painting, or scholarship, seems a hybrid partly born of both, yet partly conflicting with both in that they affirm a different order of existence altogether. But for Spindrift, who has taken his life in his own hands, for however long and on whatever terms, there is still "plenty of time."

4. A CLOCKWORK ORANGE

In 1960, back in England, Burgess began a new decade facing his own imminent death. "What's it going to be then, eh?" asks the first sentence of *Clockwork Orange*. The pressure of time always strongly felt by Burgess, became an even more significant element in his life and mind. Having practically no insurance, no savings, and with his wife having no career of her own, Burgess felt it necessary to leave her at least some financial resources. He began a period of enormous output, working steadily at the typewriter, with ideas, characters and images churning through his mind in extraordinary ways. Within 18 months he had written *six* novels to help support his wife during her widowhood. *Clockwork Orange* was the first published fruit of this new determination. Perhaps his best known book, both on its own merits and from the Stanley Kubrick film, *Orange* was a radical experiment for Burgess, and a marked departure from his previous fictional techniques. Having shown himself capable of brilliantly constructed traditional novels, Burgess turned to new novelistic sub-genres for variety, hoping at the same time to reach a wider audience.

The principle character is altogether a different sort of hero. His name is Alex—Alexander. One of the most famous pupils of Aristotle was Alexander the Great, who at sixteen became regent while his father marched against Byzantium. Alexander's razing of Thebes struck terror into all Greece. The

Alex of Burgess's novel is 15 at the start of the book, and commands his own terrorizing "army." In fact, the book has two heroes, both of them named Alexander, and they may be seen as opposite Manichean principles, though paradoxicaly they both champion the same thing in the end; like the Biblical stories which hover constantly in the background of the book, one becomes Christ while the other seeks to crucify him.

Clockwork Orange is a masterpiece as both a novel and a film, but the linguistic richness of the book is unsurpassed. The theme is a simple one, yet like most simple but profound themes it has such complexity that it cannot be unequivocally stated. Essentially, Burgess has written another variation on his Manichean dialectic, but the key issue here is freedom of choice. The book suggests that both sides of the dialectic must be allowed to survive, for without them there would be no real choice, and the world would be based on tyranny rather than freedom. The central character, Alex, seems at first to be an unalloyed embodiment of evil, violence, and Thanatos (the death principle). Yet, these traits are combined with a love for great music, which we already know to be a conventional Burgess signal for virtue, youthful vitality, good looks, wit, and a lively linguistic inventiveness. He is our "humble narrator," and since the story is told in the first person, we naturally feel somewhat close and sympathetic to Alex. His wild slang vocabulary is appealing in its novelty and its rhythms, and serves to distance us somewhat from the real horror of the "ultra-violence" he practices, preserving some room for sympathy in the reader.

Books and the act of writing are centrally important to the novel, and they amplify the theme of freedom of choice, freedom of expression. The first victim Alex and his gang attack is a reader, a man carrying books from a library. Their second violence is directed against a writer, the second "Alexander" of the book, a man who is working on a manuscript entitled *A Clockwork Orange*. In his first attack on the writer, Alex takes time to read some of the unfinished work aloud: "The attempt to impose upon man, a creature of growth and capable of sweetness, to ooze juicily at the last round the bearded lips of God, to attempt to impose, I say, laws and conditions appropriate to a mechanical creation, against this I raise my sword-pen—" Alex doesn't really fathom this, for he lives in a young physical worlds, not in the world of ideas. But by the end of the book, things have come full circle. Alex has become a writer; in fact, he is the narrator of the book we are reading, also entitled *A Clockword Orange*. And the message of Alex's book, like that of Alexander's, is a warning about the dangers of treating the world and all in it as though it were "a mechanical creation."

Alexander later calls Alex a victim of "this modern age," and in a sense he is a kind of victim from the very beginning. Like the other teenagers in this ultra-easy technological world, Alex has been brought up in a Western scientific and mechanistic philosophy which *works* (and like the historical Alexander he is in a sense the pupil of Aristotle, or as one of the other teens

mumbles on page three, caught up in "aristotle wishy washy works").
The situation is one we've encountered before—a war without a clearly
recognizable enemy: "I couldn't help a bit of disappointment at things as
they were in those days," Alex says. Nothing to fight against really. Everything as easy as kiss-my-sharries." In his clothing and patterns of speech,
Alex seems to conform to a teenage contemporary culture, but he departs
from them in his solitary appreciation of classical music. The composers he
admires are the great German masters—and behind the problems of violence, evil, and the totalitarianism of Alex's gang and the state he lashes
out against lie the mixture of great music and tyrannous evil which led Ger-
many into two world wars. After he has beaten and bloodied the writer
and his wife, Alex returns to his room and passively listens to classical
music while more images of blood and violence race through his brain.
He even experience a passive sexual climax, but just before sleep he says:
"I wanted something starry and strong and very firm, so it was J. S. Bach
I had, the Brandenburg Concerto." As he listens to this, he thinks again
"on that cottage called HOME. The name was about a clockwork orange.
Listening to the J. S. Bach, I began to pony better what that meant now, and
I thought, slooshying away to the brown gorgeousness of the starry German
master, that I would like to have tolchoked them both harder and ripped them
to ribbons on their own floor." Why does the clockwork music of Bach
cause Alex to desire even more violence? And particularly, understanding
the "Clockwork Orange" manuscript more fully, why is he inclined to rip
its author to ribbons?

The answer, though never completely clear, seems to be that Alex senses
even from the first that _he_ is the clockwork orange: he speaks hatefully of
himself as "fruit" of his mother's womb because he sees he cannot really
change that fact. By implication, he includes us in his circle, addressing us
as "brother" and educating us to his slang, and confidentially calling himself
"Your Humble Narrator" almost as though he is telling "your" story, our
story. He is conscious of himself as writer, and he seems to know what he
is doing and he is organizing the book from the very first page, when he
speaks of "this evening I'm starting off the story with." When he writes
about the problem of evil, of choice, of freedom, he sounds very nearly like
a preacher: "But, brothers, this biting of their toe-nails over what is the
cause of badness is what turns me into a fine laughing malchick. They don't
go into what is the cause of _goodness_, so why of the other shop? If lewdies
are good that's because they like it, and I wouldn't interfere with their
pleasures, and so of the other shop. And I was patronizing the other shop.
More, badness is of the self, the one, the you or me on our oddy knockies,
and that self is made by old Bog or God and is his great pride and radosty.
But the not-self cannot have the bad, meaning they of the government
and the judges and the schools cannot allow the bad because they cannot
allow the self. And is not our modern history, my brothers, the story of brave

38

malenky selves fighting these big machines? I am serious with you, brothers, over this. But what I do I do because I like to do." In fact having delivered his sermon, Alex reads a priest's message in the newspaper which tends to support his position. The preacher argues "IT WAS THE DEVIL THAT WAS ABROAD and was like ferreting his way into like young and innocent flesh, and it was the adult world that could take the responsibility for this with their wars and bombs and nonsense."

How do you fight an enemy you can't recognize? Is it books, or politics or science which has led us to this state? When the teenage gang attacks they wear masks suggesting a combined enemy: Disraeli and Henry VIII (politics); Elvis Presley (technology, commercialism and mass culture); and the poet Shelley (literature). But Alex is a solitary hero, separate from and unlike the crowd he runs with, an individual in the midst of mass society. His own gang turns on him and turns him in for a crime which has resulted in murder. At the end of the first Part, consisting of seven chapters (the seven days of creation) he relates: "I was not your handsome young Narrator any longer but a real strack of a sight, my rot swollen and my glazzies all red and my nose bumped a bit also." As they stare at him in the police station he finally admits, "I had become a thing." He finally has been beaten into submission by a clockwork state, "and I thought to myself, Hell and blast you all, if all you bastards are on the side of the Good then I'm glad I belong to the other shop." He observes at the end of the chapter that "my watch having been taken away" he no longer has any idea of the time.

The central group of seven chapters which comprise Part Two provides us our closest view of what the state itself is like in Alex's day. First of all, "going and coming I was 6655321 and not your little droog Alex not on longer." The central question of the book remains the same, and runs like a refrain through the first chapters of this second section: "What's it going to be then, eh?" and the question is part of a sermon being delivered in the jail. The prison chaplain tries to insist that even in imprisonment, the individuals still have a choice. Alex is drawn to the "prison charlie" as he calls him for several reasons. It offers him a fairly comfortable duty, and allows him to listen to "holy music by J. S. Bach and G. F. Handel" and he even begins to like the Bible: "I read all about the scourging and the crowning with thorns and then the cross veshch and all that cal, and I viddied better that there was something in it. While the stereo played bits of lovely Bach I closed my glazzies and viddied myself helping in and even taking charge of the tolchocking and the nailing in. . . ."

The vocabulary Burgess uses takes on new significance in this context, particularly the limited words for seeing—the technological word "viddied," borrowed from the video of television; and the "glazzies" for "eyes," suggesting both glazed and glassey. Alex's brain, his freedom, his ability to choose, will be manipulated technologically through his eyes, through the "sinny," the slang word for cinema. The state inflicts the "sinny" on Alex, and the prison chaplain delineates the problems with the behavioral conditioning Ludovico Technique Alex wants to try because it seems to be his only means of escape from prison: "The question is whether such a technique can really make a man good. Goodness comes from within, 6655321. Goodness is something chosen. When a man cannot choose he ceases to be a man."

But Alex is trapped. In the outside world he seemed condemned to be good, for if he did choose to be bad his freedom would be taken away. In the inside world of the prison, there is even smaller room for choice. The only way out is this brainwashing, and though Alex tries to console himself and the chaplain with his lame remark, "it will be nice to be good, sir," the chaplain replies, "It may be horrible to be good." He continues: "You are passing now to a region where you will be beyond the reach of the power of prayer. A terrible terrible thing to consider. And yet, in a sense, in choosing to be deprived of the ability to make an ethical choice, you have in a sense really chosen the good. So I shall like to think." Alex is moving into a moral and political realm larger than anything he can understand, and we increasingly come to recognize his innocence. In fact, his trust of his fellow gang-members had led to his arrest in Part One, and the pattern is repeated as his cellmates blame a murder on him in Part Two. Alex remembers the earlier betrayal as he ponders, "There was no trust anywhere in the world. O my brother, the way I could see it."

Alex does not see things clearly though; he is a member of a generation not allowed to see, but forced to "viddy" and "glazz," and in choosing the Ludovico technique he makes the innocent mistake of trusting the State. His innocence is only accentuated as he ponders the silliness of the officials thinking they can make him good merely by having him watch "sinnys": "I had a real horrorshow smeck at everybody's like innocence." As they wire him into place, he symbolically is subjected precisely to an exaggerated form of the very State treatment he delineated when he complained "There was nothing to fight against really." They make him completely passive, wire him to various machines, inject him with drugs, and force him to watch "A very good like professional piece of sinny". This is essentially the posture the State has adopted for all its inhabitants, forcing them to be dependent upon machines, giving them drugs (the milkbar of the neighborhood tavern), feeding them sinny doses of vicarious excitement. Alex doesn't realize the devastating commentary he makes on society when he innocently observes, "It's funny how the colours of the like real world only seem really real when you viddy them on the screen."

Burgess raises a very large question about violence in the media. And the painful probing of the question arises even more obviously in Kubrick's violent film. In Burgess's work we are constantly *aware* of violence as a moral problem. But in much of the professional fare shown in movie houses and on television today (with the approval of the State), the violence is present in detail *without* the moral questioning. Again, Alex is both innocent and acute as he reacts to the films the State makes him watch: "This was real, very real, though if you thought about it properly you couldn't imagine lewdies actually agreeing to having all this done to them in a film, and if these films were made by the Good or the State, you couldn't imagine them being allowed to take these films. . . ." The State is not really concerned with "Good" so much as with Expedient. They will chemically train Alex to be sick at violence without themselves seeking to eliminate the causes of the violence or to strengthen moral understanding. In fact, they have evidently condoned violence in the making of the films, and they are later shown to have purposefully hired the traitorous killers in Alex's former gang as policemen, to conduct regular raids, and beat and maul the citizenry. The violence committed upon Alex by the treatment is that of the mind-snatcher: they so completely rob Alex of choice that he is even afraid of his own sleeping mind, and can only contemplate suicide. By turning Alex even against the music which was his one private pleasure, they make the "innocent" 16-year-old begin to recognize what he is up against: "I don't mind about the ultra-violence and all that cal. I can put up with that. But it's not fair on the music. It's not fair I should feel ill which I'm slooshying lovely Ludwig van and G. F. Handel and others. All that shows you're an evil lot of bastards and I shall never forgive you, sods." As he says himself, he has become a clockwork orange. Time has run out and has no meaning for him—the State has seized his watch, and with it complete control: "Oh my brothers and friends, it was like an age. It was like the beginning of the world to the end of it." We have come from the Genesis of Part One, through the destruction of Part Two, to "Orange," the omega, the end.

When the prison chaplain witnesses the transformed Alex he continues his objections: "He ceases also to be a creature capable of moral choice"; but the State replies, "These are subtleties. . . We are not concerned with motive, with the higher ethics." The State is clearly the real author of the clockwork orange, and the Ludovico Plan encapsulates and symbolizes the worst features of state control. The Minister of the Inferior, as Alex has appropriately called him, is proud that "it works." The prison charlies sigh, "it works all right, God help the lot of us."

Part Three recapitulates and resolves the themes of the first two parts. The resolution is accomplished not so much in direct action or commentary as in the fact that Alex providentially is led through a number of highly significant returns. He attempts to go back to his parents but finds he has been replaced by a stranger, a lodger, who because he is a stranger and a lodger merely without making the demands of a son, actually suits them better; he is beaten and kicked by the old book-carrying man he had attacked in the first chapter, and this merciless retaliation shows the victim to be no better than the attacker; he is "rescued" by the police, members of his old gang who take him out in the country and beat him to a bloody pulp; and finally, barely conscious and helpless to fight back now that the State has conditioned him, he drags himself to a door he had entered once before at the cottage called "HOME" where the writer Alexander, author of *A Clockwork Orange*, lives.

Alexander likens Alex to his own wife, whom Alex's gang had raped and killed, as "a victim of the modern age." He echoes the chaplain's morality: "A man who cannot choose ceases to be a man," and protests, "To turn a decent young man into a piece of clockwork should not, surely, be seen as any triumph for any government, save one that boasts of its repressiveness." He rightly observes, "you have been sent here by Providence," but the reader soon learns that even this supposedly disinterested author, claiming to help Alex, is motivated from personal considerations as well as political objectives, and not out of genuine altruism. Alexander slowly begins to suspect that Alex may have had something to do with his wife's assault, but in any case his desire to *use* Alex (or possibly some motive of revenge, or both) prompts him to torture the boy by playing classical music to him in a locked room. Driven mad, Alex jumps from the window in an attempted suicide, but undergoes a final resurrection.

The State evidently regains control, but due to all the adverse publicity they put Alex back in his former self, and even plan to give him a job. Yet despite appearances at the end, Alex is a different person from the one who began. Throughout his story, Alex refers to his head as his "gulliver," and there are many similarities between this book and Swift's *Gulliver's Travels*. Parts One and Two are in some ways like the voyages to Lilliput and Brobdinag—both are distortions, one little (the individual Alex and his gang of three) and one large (the State, the culture). And at the end Alex, like Gulliver, must decide whether to hate all types of men, all types of behavior, or whether to make a final leap of trust or of faith. Alex is curiously Christian in his surrender: "Waiting to have done to me what was going to be done to me, because I had no plans for myself, O my brothers." And he is finally, in effect, crucified, dead, buried, and resurrected—but because the resurrection has been arranged by the State, it is a secular maneuver, not a moral triumph. Alexander is imprisoned, and Alex sells out to the State system, shaking hands with the Minister of the Interior, (a position which has come to apply to the interior of one's brain!), and goes back to living in the acceptably violent reality society had first produced in him.

Unfortunately, the American edition of *Clockwork Orange* deletes the final and seventh chapter of the last part and thereby destroys the symmetry of this Manichean trilogy. Burgess says in his *Paris Review* interview, "I hate having two versions of the same book. . . . [In the U.S. edition] the arithmological plan is messed up. Also, the implied view of juvenile violence as something to go through and then grow out of is missing in the American edition; and this reduces the book to a mere parable, whereas it was intended to be a novel. . . . In Chapter 21 Alex grows up and realizes that ultraviolence is a bit of a bore, and it's time he had a wife and a malensky googoogooing malchickiwick to call him dadada. This was meant to be a mature conclusion, but nobody in America has ever liked the idea." Partly, this must be because we hate to see Alex lose his individualism; his maturity is a final sell-out to the State. The modern age is morally condemned while Alex becomes an unresisting part of it. It is a truer story this way, a dystopian vision perfectly in line with the view of the modern super-state Burgess puts forward in the same interview: "All governments are evil."

A Clockwork Orange forces us to examine politics, media, and morality, and to ask what kind of fruit we have grown from "the world-tree in the world-orchard that like Bog or God planted." The action is not so far from the arbitrary violence currently occurring in the large cities of the world. In fact, this is a kind of disorder which has always been with us.

As Alexander puts Alex in an apartment for safe keeping while orchestrating his moves against the political establishment, his friend da Silva tells him: "Rest, rest, perturbed spirit," a remark Hamlet makes to his father's ghost as he discovers something rotten in Denmark. In Shakespeare's play, Hamlet concludes the brief speech by lamenting, "The time is out of joint:—O cursed spite,/That ever I was born to set it right!" Alex is no Hamlet. He is more like the restless ghost who haunts our conscience with his message that our time is out of joint. The clockwork orange state is a rotten mechanical fruit, but on Alex, a ghost who will not be put to rest, Burgess pins the hope that this disturbed spirit may somewhere awaken our sleeping moral sensibilities, that someone will step forth truly to set the time to right.

5. THE WANTING SEED

It is not unreasonable to expect to find strong stylistic, thematic, and generic links between novels written in close proximity, and this is certainly the case with the trio of futuristic fictions Burgess produced in rapid short order. Though published first, *Clockwork Orange* was the last of these in order of composition. It was written in the first half of 1961, while *The Wanting Seed* was completed between August and October in 1960, and *One Hand Clapping* in November and December, 1960. Taken together, the three form a counterpart of the Malayan Trilogy which we might call a dystopian trilogy, though Burgess has never indicated they should be read together or in any particular sequence. *Seed* and *Orange* are most closely related, both having futuristic settings, while *Hand* brings the problems more specifically home to contemporary England.

Seed contains the kernel of *Orange*, as the organic metaphor suggests. It is concerned with the germ, the problem of conception—a familiar problem in Burgess's work from the time he named his first heroine Concepcion. While Burgess never seems to repudiate the newspaper article in *Orange* which caused Alex to declare, "It was the adult world that could take the responsbility for this with their wars and bombs and nonsense," he explores that notion fully in this novel. We are dealing here with the adult world, and the book opens with a bereaved mother—Beatrice-Joanna—weeping over the tidy yellow plastic coffin which contains the remains of her son, remains which the Ministry of Agriculture will work back into the soil to help replenish the world's dwindling mineral resources. Society, overpopulated and unable to support its excess millions, has strictly limited the numbers of offspring allowed each parent, and encouraged homosexuality as one way of battling fertility. The death of this boy is welcomed by the State, because it is one less mouth to feed. "Try to be sensible. Try to be modern. . . . Leave motherhood to the lower orders, as nature intended," they argue with her. The old fashioned impulse to generate is out of place in the future, and the adult world is as much at a loss as Alex in knowing how to deal with it. Like Alex at the end of *Orange*, Beatrice-Joanna can say merely, "I'll never forgive you." The phrase runs as an anti-Christian litany through both of these dystopian works. With the State replacing God, the Christian virtue of forgiveness becomes mere foolishness.

The city of London has swallowed up the isles; the population is racially hybrid, a mixture of the colonies come home to roost: "Eurasian, Euro-African, Euro-Polynesian predominated." Presiding over a society determined to propogate sterility and non-procreative sex is a statue of Pelagius; and atop the Ministry of Infertility is "a naked sexless figure breaking eggs." We might recall the final interview between Alex and the State psychiatrist in *Orange*: the young doctor shows him a photograph of a bird nest full of eggs, and asks "And what would you like to do about it?" Alex replies: "Smash them. Pick up the lot and like throw them against a wall or a cliff or something and then viddy them all smash up real horrorshow." The doctors, representative of the State, reply in unison, "Good, good." Beatrice-Joanna, like Joanna in the Bible who visits Jesus's tomb and finds it empty, is overwhelmed by grief, and in her sorrow she becomes, like the early Christians, a force to be reckoned with. First, she looks upon the sea as an ancient symbol of fertility, and offers up a pagan prayer: "Sea, help us. We're sick, O sea. Restore us to health, restore us to life." And in the more rational part of her brain, as one of the rare surviving specimens of pure English descent: "Was it, she thought in an instant almost of prophetic power, to be left to her and the few indisputable Anglo-Saxons like her to restore sanity and dignity to the mongrel world? Her race, she seemed to remember, had done it before."

Beatrice-Joanna, whose name combines Dante's divine vision of Beatrice with the Biblical Joanna, and suggests the heroic Joan of Arc, is willing to take upon herself the task Hamlet recognizes when he sees that time is out of joint, and realizes that it is his mission to set it right again. Though B-J feels the stirrings of a call to action, she is not certain how to begin. Not only must she reverse the sterile brainwashing of the State, she must also make sense of her feelings for two men, her husband Tristram and her brother-in-law and lover Derek (her husband's brother). Counting the elevator floors to her apartment, B-J reveals her confusion in temporal and organic terms reminiscent of *Clockwork Orange*: something seems rotten to her since the death of her son, and as she thinks of Tristram's body, it seems as if it "had become carrion; that of his elder brother was fire and ice, paradisaical fruit, inexpressibly delicious and exciting. She was in love with Derek, she decided, but she did not think she loved him. 30—31—32. She loved, she decided, Tristram, but was not in love with him. So, so far hence in time, a woman contrived to think with (as it was in the beginning) her instincts, (is now) her complicated nerves, and (ever shall be) her inner organs (world without end) 39-40. (Amen.)" She is in touch with an organic inner clarity that promises hope, and Burgess conveys it beautifully in this poetic-religious passage.

The two men are quite different from one another. Tristram is a boys school teacher of Modern History. He recites a lesson to his pupils in chapter two, explaining "The gradual subsumption of the two main opposing political ideologies under essentially theologico-mythical concepts." These are Pelagianism, after Pelagius, "man of the sea," and Augustinianism. Pelagius "denied the doctrine of Original Sin and said that man was capable of working out his own salvation. . . . all this suggests human perfectability. Pelagianism was thus seen to be at the heart of liberalism and its derived doctrines, especially Socialism and Communism." Pelagius's doctrines are cyclical opposition to Augustinianism: "Augustine, on the other hand, had insisted on man's inherent sinfulness and the need for his redemption through divine grace. This was seen to be at the bottom of Conservatism and other *laissez-faire* and non-progressive political beliefs." He diagrams the progression of these tendencies as cyclical recurrences in "a sort of perpetual waltz, Pelphase, Interphase, Gusphase, Interphase, Pelphase," and insists that "We are both God and the Devil, though not at the same time." Another corollary of the talk is interesting in light of Alex's behavior in *Orange*: "Only the disappointed resort to violence." Alex is a disappointed Pelagian, full of a sense of perfectibility.

Derek, on the other hand, works for the propaganda department of the Ministry of Infertility. He poses as a homo in order to maintain his up-and-coming career, and expects a major promotion soon; but he is desperately concerned that someone (particularly a suspicious character named Loosely) may uncover his heterosexual interest in B-J. A far more contradictory character than Tristram, even at the beginning, Derek drops his homo guise as soon as he is alone in the apartment with B-J, and makes love with her (though she doesn't tell him she hasn't taken contraceptives). She points out the contradiction that he should "love love" but be ashamed of it, and he shrugs it off easily: "Contradictions. Instincts tell us one thing and reason tells us another. That could be tragic if we allowed it to be. But it's better to see it as comic. We were right. . . to throw God out and install Mr. Livedog in his place. God's a tragic conception."

At the very time Derek is telling B-J of the dangers of God, Tristram has encountered a defrocked priest who still believes in the old religion. Disconcerted by the news that he will not receive a promotion (because of the "aura of fertility" that surrounds him), heterosexual Tristram leaves his class early, and goes to a bar where the priest tells him: "Man needs divine grace." The Cleric insists "Unfrocked. . . . .But they can never take away this power, never, never." On the way home Tristram notices newly unemployed youngsters being taken into the police, ruffians a la *Orange*. The government is getting tough and insistent, and is planning to crack down on the bands of violent hoodlums and on those who violate the fertility laws. They are entering an Augustinian phase (Gusphase).

The chapters of Part one are counterpointed against one another in a fast-paced varied prelude. The contrasting occupations of the male characters—politics and education—allow great diversity in point of view, and making Tristram a teacher offers a convenient way to educate the reader on the rather obscure attributes of Pelagianism and Augustinianism. The language, though it contains far less slang than *Orange*, does show the beginnings of a specialized argot. The characters are clearly drawn, the plotting is swift and sure, and the dialogue is lively and convincing. Tristram and Derek encounter each other in the elevator, one coming, one going, and Derek makes lame excuses for being there. Home at last, Tristram ends the evening by making love to his wife, thereby missing the Prime Minister's announcement on television that the government has declared war against lawlessness. Derek has been named Metropolitan Commissioner of the Population Police, and a strike has been settled by a new police unit named "greyboys, using truncheons and carbines, laughing the while; a splash of chromatic brains on the camera lens" like something out of *Orange*.

Homosexuality is a continuing presence in Burgess's work, and in this book perhaps more than any of the earlier novels it becomes a human metaphor for a contrived reality at odds with "nature"—what at one time we might have called the "natural order of God's creation." In *Battlements* Ennis found sanctuary with his homosexual roommate, and even in this first book sexual inversion seemed to be a blessedly sane response to the insanity of arbitrarily enforced authority and macho bureaucracy. In *Orange* Alex apparently reclaims at least a portion of his identity when he asserts his masculinity against inverted aggressive sexual attack in the jail, but the violence of his response, and his conventional sexual preference oddly enough put him directly in touch with the values and morals of the State. From that point until the end of the book, where Alex apparently "wins," he also increasingly sells out to conventionality, and follows a path similar to those of his former "droogs"-turned-state-police. This point is made even clearer in the original ending to the book, the 21st chapter expurgated from American versions of the book. In *Seed* Burgess makes clear that homosexuality is valuable not in and of itself, but metaphorically as an outpost of individualism. When the state declares it necesary that everyone be homosexual, only the heterosexual has a chance at real individualism. This is a significant metaphoric tool throughout Burgess's fiction, used most conspicuously in *Honey For the Bears*, the book published immediately following *Orange* (and written in the second half of 1961).

The homosexual and heterosexuasl extremes are presented exclusively from a male perspective. They form the boundaries of the cycle, the extreme manifestations of opposites which correspond to pelphase and gusphase. Moreover they are conjoined to the occupations—politician and educator—which have so frequently been prominent in the Burgess canon. What could be a mere shadow play of black and white extremes is given complexity through comedy and satire of both positions, and through the presence of Beatrice-Joanna, probably the most complex female character thus far in Burgess, and one who connects the book to forces of natural creativity, individual will, instinctual behavior, and religious impulse. Her independent spirit refuses to accept the finality of death at the beginning of the book, and she does not blindly accept either of the extremes represented by her two lovers. Interestingly enough, she finally gives birth to twins, an action which seems to vindicate through her body the presence of both of them. The twins are unexpected, like so much of B-J's behavior; Burgess affirms and applauds this unpredictable quality. While Derek is trapped by his own position, Tristram by his intellectual postures and self absorption wallows in his fate: "What worse betrayal could there be than this? Betrayal by wife. Betrayal by brother. Oh, Dog, Dog, Dog." His universe becomes a prison even before he is literally jailed: "The whole crowded street, the sky, had become his own betrayed home, a cell of suffering."

B-J excapes from the city, seeking State Farm NW313, where her sister Mavis and brother-in-law Shonny live. They offer her a sanctuary long enough to give birth, and Shonny delivers the twins with his veterinarian's hands, but they are clearly as limited in their rustic extremity as the other extremes of the novel. What comes frighteningly clear in the book is the uncertainty of the clockwork universe. A brief scene with Prime Minister Robert Starling reminds us of the assertion we nearly all tacitly accept: "The history of man is the history of his control over his environment." But the environment in *Seed*—political, physical, intellectual, religious, and emotional environment—is out of control. At the beginning of Part Three the world faces a "blight never known before." There are massive crop failures and death stalks the world in every nook. The phase begins to shift again; when reason fails the world turns predictably to superstition. The reversal seems focused on Shonny s he delivers B-J's children. The plague has hit even his small home, but as he prepares this delivery, his heart, for some reason, is lifted in tremendous elation. "Of course. *there* was the big secret—all life was one, all life was one."

' There is a truth to Shonny's remark. B-J's birth act seems almost to reverse the plague. The sow nearly dead in the barn suddenly recovers, the crops begin to sprout again, the people begin copulating in the fields in a kind of sympathetic magic. Yet Burgess is not affirming Shonny's simplistic truth. All life is one, he says; yet still he delivers *twins*. The act of birth seems to be a good omen, but Mavis turns on her sister and wants her out of the house. In fact, the birth of the twins seems to have a direct though obscure connection to the death of Shonny's own children. And, finally, we see Shonny, who has upheld the old religion and the old ways throughout the time of plague and hardship, bitterly turning against his religion and renouncing it in despair and anger.

Time affords a shifting ground for reality. Any fixed points seem doomed to disaster, and Shonny's assertions, however we may find them instinctively sympathetic, are as fixed and therefore as uncertain as Derek's. A more positive index for survival turns out to be motion, mobility, and change—the characteristics of the sea B-J so instinctively admires. Derek is a fixed point, caught in his own political nets; Shonny is fixed agriculturally outside the urban sprawl. Tristram appears to be locked inside his own mind for much of the book, with only B-J capable of the essential mobility; but finally Tristram does begin to move.

Tristram's escape from prison is reminiscent of Spindrift's escape from the hospital in *The Doctor is Sick*. When it actually happens, he finds it extremely simple—one of the important messages in Burgess appears to be that the individual can change his situation largely through desire. One just needs to make up his mind. So Tristram merely walks out. However, at the very time Tristram is making good his escape, B-J and her sister Mavis are engaged in disagreeable petty bickering, caught up in their circumstances, and B-J crippled by lack of money, unable to get in touch with Tristram, with nowhere else to go. At the same time, Mavis is acutely aware that her sister's presence is constantly endangering her own children, and there is even some competition for Shonny's favor present. Before they can resolve the issue, Captain Loosely arrives, having tracked them down at last, and B-J surrenders herself and the twins, explaining, "it looks as though the future's taken care of. It seems that I've found somewhere to go."

Part Four follows Tristram across the country as he travels to the farm where he hears his wife has been staying. During the journey he has an opportunity to see just how far society has changed. He learns to share the human flesh now readily available from the various "dining clubs," and participates in some of the "Dionysian revels," heterosexual, of course, which are now commonplace in the fields and streets; and he learns that the government is regrouping, with the Ministry of Infertility removing the "in" prefix and changing its approach. The new prime minister, George Ockham, appears on the television to promise "the good life with a minimum of State interference," clearly showing a new cycle "in the true Augustinian manner"—the Gusphase. Yet, by giving his Prime Minister the name of a post-Augustinian philosopher, Burgess suggests that even this may be changing.

Tristram accidentally finds himself in church, and in the midst of the service the proceedings are interrupted by shouts of protest and complaint. Shonny is cursing this new god for taking his children. Tristram follows him out, and learns from him of his wife's pregnancy and the fact that she bore twins, whom she named Derek and Tristram. He and Shonny are oddly detached from one another, each completely absorbed in their own concerns, but Tristram learns a more important lesson from their meeting. He finds himself out of sympathy with the new Augustinianism, and can condemn its religiosity, but in trying to console Shonny he finds himself saying: " 'You believe it's right for man to go on sinning for ever, because that way you justify your belief in Jesus Christ.' for he saw that whatever government was in power he would always be against it." This discovery echoes Burgess's own observation: "All governments are evil." In any case, Tristram finds his journey has been pointless since B-J is not there. Shonny will give him nothing in the way of money for food or transportation back to London, and Tristram wanders into a "Communal Feeding Centre" for a bowl of stew, suddenly finding himself trapped into the new army.

War seems to be the only solution society can ever find to the serious problems of human existence. This threat of violence draws a boundary of certainty and finality around the clockwork universe in many a Burgess novel. It offers an approximation of apocalypse. For good or for evil, it does have a way of defining any given situation with a certainty missing in the shifting sands of time. *Seed* began with the proposition that war had been outlawed, but the elimination of death at one end of the social and political scale had necessitated the elimination of birth at the other. At the end of the book, with the reemergence of fecundity, concimmitant war seems inevitable. As Tristram Foxe begins to comprehend his situation at the close of Part Four, he sinks into a chair, "And laughed, crying." Suddenly we are reminded of two important English Foxes who precede him: the great Quaker George Fox, the man of peace, and Fox's *Book of Martyrs*.

Part Five rapidly alters the situation, as we encounter Derek Foxe the politician, now Minister of Fertility (Loosely's scheme of revealing Derek's secret children has worked to Derek's credit in the new order!), babbling baby talk to the twins. B-J has joined him in opulent and comfortable circumstances, and the way of the world seems like the babbling of this unprincipled man: "Boo boo boo boop a doop." In fact, as always, Burgess is writing brilliant satirical comedy, with his understated references to "fish" (the regenerative image of the sea, so important to B-J) and "treadmill" (which by now suggests the repetitive cyclical nature of time by which we arbitrarily become victims or pompous asses): The twins are "bubbling like fish, secure in their play-pen, podgily clotched the rails and performed a treadmill action. Tiny Tristram alone said, like Upanishadian thunder, 'Da da da.' 'Ah,' said Derek seriously, 'we ought to have more, lots, lots more.' 'So they can put in the army and shot at?' said Beatrice-Joanna.' " The "dada" reference suggests one modern art movement, while the speaking thunder reminds us of Eliot's *Wasteland*. And Derek's babytalk climaxes with his stupidly repeating "worple, worple, worple," one of the nonsense words from "Jabberwocky." At least B-J still has some sense of the nonsensical treadmill: "Sex. War and sex. Babies and bullets." Derek wants her to marry him, and insists Tristram must have been killed and eaten; but B-J clings to her intuitions and still insists, "I like things to be right, that's all." For her that seems to mean: "two men in her life."

Trapped in the war machine, Tristram is promoted to sergeant, but grows increasingly suspicious of the war; and in his capacity as education officer is sympathetic to doubts and questions about fighting. As a penalty for his doubts, he is sent to the front, where he discovers it is a deadly serious "gramophony" war being used as a device to kill off manflesh which can be cooked, canned, and fed to the people. Although only an exaggerated version of the economics of any conflict, it is still a horrifying image in its naked form. Tristram, once he has recognized the truth, feigns death on the battlefield and thus escapes once again. He simply walks out, walks out of the other side of the field in Ireland where the battle is being staged, amazed that it is "going to be easy." As in other situations, once the illusions are pierced, you are all but out.

Tristram has seen the enemy, and it is *us*. He goes to the war department, intending to blow the whistle, but finds the "War Dept." is actually a private corporation not subject to government control, and recognizes his powerlessness. In the end he merely accepts his old profession of teacher (and certainly he has something more to teach now—with greater authority and purposefulness, though probably without any greater effect). In the final pages, he once again finds B-J, as she is facing the sea: "And she prayed for someone, and the prayer was at once answered, but the answer did not come from the sea. It came from the warmer land behind her. A gentle hand on her arm." In their final embrace, Burgess affirms something more than mere expediency. Between them there is something larger than a physical connection, operating at the level of intuition, a dimension which for Tristram since leaving that death field has been on a transcendent level, or as Burgess put it: "A whole slab of time somehow outside time."

The concluding words of the epilog are partly a prayer, partly a benediction: "The wind rises. . . we must try to live. The immense air opens and closes my book. The wave, pulverized, dares to gush and splatter away from the rocks. Fly away, dazzled, blinded pages. Break, waves. Break with joyful waters. . . . " More hopeful than *Clockwork Orange*, *Seed* suggests there is a chance for survival, and even for a positive answer to B-J's prayer "Sea. . . teach us all sense." Tristram the teacher at the end of the book has walked through death and back to life, with knowledge and vision enriched. Burgess successfully walked the same road through this shadow of death, completing his five novels, and miraculously surviving the death sentence his doctors had pronounced. His teaching and his sense seem to have come clearer for it, and both of these have been sharpened by an awareness of time.

6. ONE HAND CLAPPING

The zen title of this comic and materialistic novel is only one irony of many in its deceptively simple framework. It promises a philosophical perspective with an Eastern flavor, but merely delivers a miasma of Western materialism and violence. It does truthfully refer, however, to a lack of thesis-antithesis. In fact, the attempt to resist the single-moded value system is as vain a pursuit, Howard learns, as one hand clapping. Who is the enemy, where is the enemy? There is nothing to come up against in this novel (a fact Alex later complains about in *Clockwork Orange*), except oblivion.

The story is narrated by Janet Shirley, 23, a horribly unimaginative product of the welfare estate living in a government housing project. Husband Howard Shirley works as a used car salesman; Janet works in a supermarket: "We had a TV, a radio with a strap like a handbag for carrying round the house, a washing-machine, a vac, but no car of our own or children." This inventory of her life reveals the emptiness of the middle class structure she inhabits. De Vitis points out: "The language of the novel is hers, and Burgess carefully and brilliantly forces it to yield the essential meaning of his piece." It is another masterpiece of first person narrative, limited in this case to the mundane and trivial vocabulary of an uneducated woman who understands little of what she sees. It succeeds masterfully not only in evoking the emptiness of life in the welfare state, but in conveying the appalling consequences of vacuity. Janet's narrative is a mirror in words of her husband's problem, which in turn mirrors a larger societal problem. Howard is remarkable in no way except that he possesses a photographic memory. He can repeat *verbatim* detailed bits of information, but he never comprehends the real significance of any of it, never attains an *understanding* of his own. In other words, in the terms of the title, he has one hand only; there can never be any contact of hand against hand, mind against mind. Howard repeats information without understanding in much the same way that Janet repeats the events of her story without grasping its significance.

Howard at least appears to understand his "gift": "It was only a photographic brain, he called it, and he said that a lot of people had it and it meant nothing at all." Howard inhabits an entire society of mere repetition and

mimicry, symbolized in the novel through television, and through TV commercials in particular. Janet and Howard form their ideas of life from commercial images which are repeated until they are thoroughly saturated.
Janet confesses she is swayed to want children, "especially during the commercials, showing mother and daughter both protected by the same soap, or the mother loving her children so much that she washed all their clothes in Blink or whatever it was (they're all the same, really). . . ." Howard is so overwhelmed with his photographic brain being subjected to these continual, materialistic repetitions that he wants to have it all, to be a millionaire "for, say, one month," and then "to snuff it, having tasted a bit of life. Because when all's said and done, there's not all that much to live for, is there?"

Howard connects his fate with a TV quiz show called *Over and Over*, a title which emphasizes the repetitious motifs of the book. He selects the category of "books," and of course is able to spout back the answer to every question asked. With the money he wins on his first appearance, he and Janet go out for a meal, get a little drunk, and have an accident in the borrowed Bentley car Howard has taken from his lot. The next day they are both late for work, oversleeping from overindulgence and the excitement, and Howard quits his job when his boss begins to complain that "he'd lost a lot of sales because of me being too honest with the customers." Howard, we see through the shallow veneer of his wife, is essentially dedicated to truth and honesty, and is constantly horrified at the lack of these qualities in the world. In fact, "Howard was now quite famous in Bradcaster [a corruption of "broadcaster"?], and people would point him out in the street. But it didn't seem to me that they pointed him out in a *nice* way, as if he was a pop-singer, but in a sort of miced way, part admiring and part sneering. if you see what I mean, as though it was all wrong for a grown man to waste his time on book-learning. . . ."

Howard tries to seize control of his life, and to move it to the top of the materialistic heap in order to assess its value. He calls up the supermarket and tells them Janet won't be back to work, and they leave together for his final appearance on the quiz show. The entire quiz show situation seems to be an elaborate echo of the episode in *Doctor is Sick* where Spindrift finds himself in the bald-headed-man contest; here too there is a hollow aspect to his victory. Howard wins, of course, and establishes his superiority over the staff of the show by intentionally answering a question with the author's original name (Ford Maddox Heuffer rather than the more widely known Ford Maddox Ford); just for a moment, Janet has a small epiphany: "It was almost as if it was Howard himself thinking and not me, that it was cheap and dirty to applaud something that nobody had any idea of, that nobody cared a bit about these three men, whoever they were. . . dead and dignified and quiet and sort of despising everybody here in this studio. And I'd never read them or even heard of them and I felt sorry and mean somehow. . . . " Interviewed the next day by a reporter from the *Daily Window*, Howard reveals that he had a similar vision of the dead authors looking at him from their graves, "looking at me, sort of sadly, sort of in sadness and pity." He has sensed a significance in the older, humanistic writers, the possibility of a dignity and idealism negated by mass culture, and he has enough shreds of his own sensibilities remaining to recognize that these great authors were "Humiliated at school where we had to do them, *The Mill on the Floss* and *A Shorter Boswell* and *Henry IV Part I*. . . and we drew dirty drawings all over them. And the teachers were no better than we were. And now humiliated by just being used to win a thousand pounds. And humiliated by you, too." The reporter represents the new "literature," which according to Howard is "Full of 'I guess' and 'right now' and pandering to teenagers." It appeals to the lowest common denominator and is designed merely to sell, not to educate, elevate, inspire, or question. It is literature mired in the present, content with what is, complacent in the status quo.

Nearly all manifestations of time in *One Hand* take this temporary form: no past or future, but present, material, static, and transient. Howard alone seems inclined to break this tyranny of complacent present time. His feeling that the literary past is being degraded in the present shows that he has at least a faint understanding of history, and his inclination to plan a future for himself—and one which *he* will determine through his own choices and actions (rather than merely allowing present events to take their course and define the future for him)—bespeaks his impulse toward transcendence. Howard alone among the characters in this book feels discontent with the conventional acceptance of time. He won't be governed by it; he has, for example, real difficulty on the quiz program in learning to obey the time rules: "He was told he must *wait* thirty seconds before giving his answer."

Howard proposes to train his photographic mind to leap into the future: "This is the hard part. What I have to imagine now is this *Cope's Race-goer's Encyclopedia* for next year. What I have to close my eyes and see now is this page with all the winners for all the different years and this year's winner [of a race which hasn't yet been run] at the end of the list." It involves the radical assumption that a mind can accurately imagine the future, and suggests that even an "average" mind is, or can be, *prophetic*, and *correctly* prophetic! Howard thinks he has attained this transcendence when he comes up with the name Dalnamein. Janet and Howard watch the race on television, and through their snowy reception they see his vision of the future come true. Burgess makes masterful use of his limited first person narrator at this turning point, allowing Janet to fall into unconscious imitation of the race announcer's voice. Janet's description is at once revealing of her personality, resonant with nearly religious overtones, (he sounds to her like a parson), and poetically suggestive: "Dalnamein was challenging and Windyedge was coming up and they were into the final furlong and

Dalnamein had taken the lead and was holding on and it was Windyedge just behind and Dalnamein held on and then there was the winning post and Dalnamein had beaten Windyedge by a neck, as they call it, and Howard and I didn't know whether to jump in the air and smash all the furniture or just pass out, sort of numb. What I said was: 'I think I'll go and make a cup of tea.' And I went off and did it and Howard switched the telly off and just say there looking at its big square creamy eye which was blind, with his mouth open." The television, metaphor for the electric present, is blind because it sees neither past or future. Howard has recognized himself fully as a man cognizant of the weight of history, awesome at the accurate projections the past casts upon the future.

Howard's full reaction is difficult to understand, for we see the impact of his breakthrough through Janet's limited understanding. Janet is to continue saying that there is nothing particularly remarkable or original about his mental feats, and even echoes the reporter's suggestion that it is a kind of deformity. Nonetheless, Howard has achieved something truly different. His mental step into the future may presuppose a temporal matrix of repetition. He may merely have achieved the recognition that the future will be like the past—enough like the past to be predictable. But the realization is singular, exceptional, and on at least one level, profound. He has taken his own life in his hands and changed it, shaped it to his choice. The fact that he alone, more dramatically than any other character in the book, has seized control of his own destiny, is especially remarkable in the midst of the standardized, unimaginative mass culture personified devastatingly in the very same quiz program he first bested. He has clearly demonstrated that a man has a choice, and that his mind—even his "photographic" mind—can comprehend and thus predict the future with reasonable accuracy.

His plans are generally keen and perceptive. He shows confidence and determination in the face of the unfamiliar, and makes some good choices of character. His decision to give his quiz show prize to a worthy and struggling young writer brings him in touch with an admirer who addresses him as "Mr. Shirley, patron of the arts" and adds, "I wanted to say that you did the right thing with your money, Mr. Shirley." Though his expression comes from a situation involving great deal of self-interest, Redvers Glass speaks the truth. The meeting occurs in the center of the book, and it is as though reality has stepped into a mirror, a "Reversed Glass." The two men, connected apparently by fate, like the paired Derek and Tristram, are reflections of one another. Redvers is writing the story of his life; Howard commissions him to write about death. Redvers the poet is more fully physical and sensual; Howard is almost purely mental, detached from the very material world he is seeking almost scientifically to explore. His final detachment from material existence is fully realized in his intention to physically annihilate both Janet and himself; both Janet and Redvers show themselves fond of the material world (it was money which brought Redvers into Howard's life, but for Howard their meeting was an act of generosity). They survive by flaunting mundanity.

But Redvers enters Howard's life dead-drunk, unconscious, a physical weight difficult for a policeman and Howard to carry together up the stairs. Self-centered, completely out of touch with reality, unconscious, the writer makes rough love to Janet next morning, and when Howard tries to send him on his way, admits: "They won't have me in the ancestral mansion of Sir Percival Glass, knight." His father, whose namesake was a legend in Arthurian romance, is disappointed in the son so far from the true quest of Percivale, the Grail Hero, forthright, simple, uncorrupted, pure of heart. Howard is far closer to the Percivale archetype than Redvers. These mirror images of man are both reflected most clearly through the common surface of Janet.

De Vitis, whom I think misses Howard's depth by dubbing him flatly "insane," does clearly and correctly observe: "Janet is to date Burgess's most fully developed female character, and his handling of her psychology is admirable." We watch her fall from mass-managed middle class innocence into a physical consciousness at once depressing and pitiful. Even in her "fall" she retains our sympathy for the honesty and innocence of each step: "Oh, Howard was very nice to have in bed, but he was very gentle all the time, and there was something in me that didn't want this gentleness." It is a second epiphany parallel to that moment when she found herself haunted by her husband's moral scruples during the quiz program, this time on a physical rather than spiritual plane: "And he sort of held his arms out, almost pleading, and then before I knew where I was I was sort of on the bed and he was tearing at me, very excited and sort of panting, "Oh, God, oh, God." Redvers with his arms out emblematically parodies a religious transfiguration, and the reader is bound to be sympathetic to Janet's gasp of self-recognition when she gasps "His beard was very rough and when he pressed his mouth on to mine I expected to get all the beer and drink he'd had the night before, but his breath was quite sweet. . . ."

Howard wants Janet to have a mink coat from the best furrier, Einstein's, and sends her there when he makes his offer of the death ode commission to Redvers and it's through this ruse that she meets Redvers at the Swinging Lamp, another image like the mirror that swings two ways. Janet is teased by the name Einstein's, "which is a very famous name in things other than furs but I can't think what." Howard is offering her a post-Einsteinian consciousness, awareness of relativity and time as a dimension; Redvers lures her away from that attraction to the Swinging Lamp. Janet chooses a timeless present, a blankness like the blind eye of the television set; but as she enters her pitiful timeless oblivion, she wins us with her candid account: "First of all I felt ashamed and guilty about Howard, but then this that was going on became far more important than any of those feelings.

I just wanted him, that was all, and what I wanted he wanted, too. He did everything right without selfishness. . . .'' Her climatic epiphany is not perception but oblivion: ''They often talk about time standing still, but I always thought it was just a saying and didn't mean anything, but I should have thought days and days or at least hours went by, but it was less than half an hour from start to finish.'' Perhaps she is the realistic Einsteinian, turning relativity (the mink coat) to practical use; she comes through her first full round with Redvers and as she looks ''at the lovely oyster watch Howard had bought me. . . it was only twenty to one. I'd be in nice time to heat up a tinned steak and kidney pudding and boil some potatoes and we could have lunch at the usual time.''

As more of Janet's personality emerges, prompted by the intensity of her experiences with this would be poet, her character is deepened by him, and she increasingly defines the position of both Howard and Redvers, for she reveals her limitations with each forward realization: ''I find this very hard to explain, but when you're with a man like that he isn't a man any more, he's just a lot of sounds and a smell and a weight on you. I used to think that remembering things [what Howard can do so well with his 'photographic' mind, and what Janet has herself already remarkably demonstrated in her uncanny ability to narrate all the details of her life, including the tin of beans she fixed for lunch, on precisely which day, and at which time, all the names and odds of all the horses Howard bet on, and all the questions and answers he gave on the quiz program] was really a matter of your brain, but this time it was parts of the body that kept on remembering. I was now sort of split and I knew it would be very dangerous to let my feelings run away with me. . . .I mean, there's little enough in this life, really, and you only find it worthy living for the odd moments, and if you think you're going to be able to have those odd moments again, then it makes life wonderful and have a meaning.'' She even links herself in her own mind with Juliet, and wishes she'd been able to read Shakespeare's *Romeo and Juliet* in school, or had sampled Byron, and come to an understanding of what the physical romantic was like. She'd been tied up instead with a spiritual romantic unable to comprehend her own compulsions to the mundane.

To give Howard his due, Burgess makes it clear that he is trying to bring both worlds to Janet. He has gotten enough money to ''go as high as it was possible to go,'' and having put her materially in the best hotel room in London, bought her the best vintage champagne (which she finds ''a bit vinegary''), he tries to take her to the theater, to ''a play dealing with the decay and decadence in the world about us, very witty,'' a play called *One Hand Clapping*. He tries to explain the non-materialistic suggestions it embodies, the Zen Buddhism embodied in its title: ''It's something you have to try and imagine. . . . It's a way of getting in touch with Realing, you see, proceeding by way of the absurd. . . . Like imagining thunder with no noise and a bird flying with no body or head or wings. It's supposed to be a way of getting to God." The conclusion of chapter 16, with Janet's simple reflections dispelling the apparently genuine and impressive religious grasp Howard is seeking, is one of the points in the book where Burgess makes flawless use of her narrative perspective. She allows the reader to see clearly that this play is very directly about themselves; this play within the novel conveys another perspective of relativity to their situation, and one which Janet only dimly understands: "Here we were with a lot of money, and our first night in London as very rich people had to be spent watching people in a dirty little room with washing hung up and kippers forked out on to plates. I should have been quite happy to be back in our little house in Bradcaster, sitting by the fire watching the TV. But then there was this question of Red and I was very confused. I felt that I'd sort of got on a bus going to a place I didn't know, and the bus wouldn't stop. I didn't know what I wanted. . . . I almost felt like crying with a sort of grief and hitting out at people, but plenty of that was going on on the stage."

Going on. The action of the book proceeds with reference to different planes, and hence isolated and varied perceptual planes. Howard becomes a driven man because he has chosen to time and determine his own death as he has already determined for himself his course through the world. "There's a lot to do and not all that much time," he says. On the other hand, Janet's contradictory temporal perceptions cause her to question Howard's entire matrix of values: "Why do you keep going on about not being much time? We've got all the time in the world, haven't we? [Of course, Howard recognizes that even all the world's time is a crushingly limited span.] Besides, I don't see that about a lot to do. We've done nothing since we got the money, have we? Nothing at all." Even the extraordinary departures from their former routine go unnoticed to Janet. In her inability to see beyond the present moment, a kind of timeless and disconnected (blindered) viewpoint, she is unable to conceive of an altered routine to even a purely physical "doing something." Howard knows that not only have they radically changed their lives, but they are also engaged in a metaphysical quest for testing meaning: " 'We've got to have everything that money can buy. . . . It's a sort of duty. We've got to prove that we've done everything we can do with money.' And we went on about this, getting excited, but I didn't see his point."

The point becomes clearer after they return and oust Redvers and his Bohemian friends from their flat; on Janet's birthday Howard begins to make his suicidal intentions increasingly clear by implication. He states his position: ". . . the world's a terrible place and getting worse and worse every day, and no matter how much you try to live pleasant you can't hide the fact that it's a rotten world and not worth living in." Janet protests with worldly appreciation: "Love. . . we've had love, lots of love." But Howard patiently explains, "I didn't mean love. . . . I meant like being true to the great men who've gone before us and not spitting in their poor dead faces as we have been doing. Like that quiz. . . .What I mean is a sort of betrayal. It's we who've betrayed things. We've betrayed the kind of world these men in the past had in mind, the kind of world they wanted to build. We've let them down, you and me and everybody." Janet is in some ways like Beatrice-Joanna as she intuitively affirms the physical: "I had a very strong desire all of a sudden to have a baby. I had a very powerful desire come sort of into my whole body to have a child of my own."

The marriage of instinct and intellect achieved at the conclusion of *The Wanting Seed* is denied in the title of *One Hand Clapping* and conclusively stated in the isolated ending of the book. Chapter 24 sets Janet and Howard dramatically against one another, clearly and unmovingly defining their positions. Janet will admit "It's a rotten world," but adds "It's not the world but the people that's in it. And you can't change it, you can't do anything about it. So you put up with it, that's what you do. And I put up with it." She is content in the present partly because she doesn't know the past: "It's not too bad of a world when you come to look at it. It's a better world than when those men with beards were alive." The cosmic implications of the actions Howard performs are lost on her. She sees their interaction as "a bit too much like a TV play. . . . something on the TV as far as I was concerned." Howard must finally be very specific: "We've got to be sort of witnesses, sort of martyrs. . . .Our deaths will sort of show how two decent ordinary people who'd been given every chance that money can give but no other chance, no other chance at all, how two such people felt about the horrible stinking world."

Howard's idealism is a distillation of all men's best and noblest impulses. His death is a dramatic protest, but also his final grasp for transcendence: "There's another world, very likely, and we shall be together in that other world, happy for ever, the two of us. And if there's no world afterwards we shall be at peace in the grave, lying together in eternal rest." He yearns for a testimony of faith. Janet is guided by the physical limitations of fear: "There's eternal fire and torment and doing away with yourself's a terrible thing and there's this fire and punishment for ever . . . . I don't want that. I don't want to go to hell, I want to stay alive." The divorce of these opposing views becomes complete as Janet thinks to herself: "At that moment he really stopped being Howard who I loved." Threatened with her own death she lashes out against Howard, and protects herself by killing him, clapping him on the head with a coal hammer. Her lone survival, her final blow as she lifts her hand against Howard, compounds the rich ironies of the title. Howard's idealistic dream of eternal comradeship, two arms clasped in union, is shattered; Janet alone is one hand clapping—one which in the very collision of hand against hand, value against value, must annihilate its companion. To survive it stands isolated, puzzlingly un-zen, in a seeming contradiction: for hands to truly encounter one another they risk destroying one another, and remaining one at last, each soundless and alone.

In her survival Janet proves incapable of lifting herself above complacency, self-centeredness, and an appallingly mundane imagination. The moments in the book when she nearly glimpses truths about herself which could imply transcendence are negated; her better feelings of what becomes almost selfless love for Howard are at last mere selfishness; her potential passion released by Redvers becomes mere convenience, and she contemplates taking the hammer to him as well if things don't go the way she likes. From that last true insight in the 24th chapter, Janet's potential dies into obdurate mediocrity: she ponders the neatness of the timing, and the reader can ponder the chronological organization of the book: "And another of my thoughts was that my life was very tidy as far as the actual time was concerned, because I was dying to the very day twenty-four years after I was born." One indication that it is, at last, Howard's story and not hers is that though she physically survives, the 27 chapters in the book testify to Howard's 27 years rather than her inconsequential 24. And the final word of the book is "Howard," though it comes in the shallow voice of Janet: "Poor silly Howard."

Burgess has completed another kind of circle—from the death of the woman who promised love, fecundity, and physical transcendence in his first female character, Concepcion; through the fertile and surviving promise of Beatrice-Joanna who survives in an aura of possible affirmation embraced by the metaphysical and idealistic Derek; finally to his strongest woman, Janet ("I'd always been pretty strong" she says as she takes up the coal hammer), a feminine counterpart of the isolated assertion of individualism through violence (and in this sense nearly a counterpart of Alex in *Clockwork Orange*). Janet takes up the burden of Howard's body, putting it into a Chinese camphorwood chest, preserving him in final zen-like fashion. She has fulfilled the work Howard originally commissioned Redvers to complete: she has told Howard's story eloquently and has let his protest be heard: "You could tell these council houses weren't all that well built because the whole house shook, ornaments rattling and ringing and a tea-cup coming off the shelf and cracking all white pieces on the floor beside Howard. It was like little hard flower petals for Howard."

Until the end of the book, Janet is to think of Howard's brain as being like a machine, a mechanical photographic bit of clockwork. Yet Howard is perhaps Burgess's most deeply apocalyptic character. He is not wrapped up in explanations like Derek, not debilitated by the burden of choosing from the confusion of a rotten present, like Ennis, Crabbe, or Spindrift; neither does he choose mere affirmation of the individual self as the best one can do in a rotten world, like Alex or Janet. He has seen the promise of the past and committed himself fully to the selfless transcendence of a radical alternative, becoming more the heroic Parsifal of the story and very nearly glimpsing the Grail. In these books Burgess has fully explored the social-political-temporal parameters of a clockwork universe. Particularly in these central novels, blended of science fiction, fantasy, and social satire, he has created eloquent philosophical moral studies and taken his writings to the limits of time and the universals.

7. THE CLOCKWORK ENDING

I have discussed these novels out of their order of composition, choosing instead to arrange them for critical convenience. While time, death, and the necessity of moral and ethical choice remain major themes in all of Burgess's subsequent writing, his visionary exploration of the clockwork universe is really climaxed in the writing of *A Clockwork Orange* in the first half of 1961. In *Honey for the Bears*, written in the second half of that year, he returns to a present-day setting of politics and petty affairs, exploring in other terms the appeal of materialism (honey) to the Russians (the bear), who claim to offer a political alternative. But in the remaining novel of this extremely productive period, Burgess set a new course for himself. One notices a difference immediately, even in the title of the book, for all of Burgess's other novels are titled with abstractions: *A Vision of Battlements, Right to an Answer, The Long Day Wanes, Devil of a State, Wanting Seed, Clockwork Orange, One Hand Clapping, The Doctor is Sick*. Suddenly we have a book named for a single character. Between January and April, 1960, Burgess wrote *Inside Mr. Enderby*, and in the process shifts direction to explore issues of meaning and significance, and political and social problems, from a much more intimate perspective. He has continued to deepen and enlarge the character in *Enderby Outside* (1968) and, finally, *Enderby's End*, significantly subtitled *The Clockwork Testament*. Enderby is a poet, and despite his shortcomings, enables Burgess to investigate a realistically heroic alter-ego. Despite his doubts and limitations, Enderby affirms in his own creations the visions of those bearded literary greats whose promise haunts Howard's short life. In still further novels, not discussed here, Burgess has explored the antithesis of the Clockwork universe, a universe lacking certainty, exactitude, precision; a universe not of machines and numbers (the clock) but of words; a literary universe, where words constantly mean more than one thing—a point delivered most dramatically in his extensive and sophisticated use of puns; a universe of myth, which stems from but transcends literature, just as literature transcends mortal temporality. Transcendence is achieved through giving up the search for exact significance and finality, and aesthetically embracing the richness of meaning language can convey and communicate. Language becomes a medium for communion, a medium which expresses transcendence of time beyond individual death. Books in this category (which I hope to treat fully in another Milford series monograph), include the three volumes in the Enderby saga; the fictional biography of Shakespeare, *Nothing Like the Sun*;

a fictional biography of Keats, *Abba Abba*; a fictive biography of Napoleon, *Napoleon Symphony*; the story of a student of literature, Miles Faber, whose initials form the title *M/F*; the poetic narrative *Moses*; the story of the writer in *Beard's Roman Women*; his studies of James Joyce; essays of *Urgent Copy*; the masterful survey of modern fiction, *The Novel Now;* and his commentary on and reply to George Orwell in *1985*.

The alternative to the Clockwork Universe for Burgess appears to be the world of individuals and of books. The fact that he has produced fine literature so prolifically is in itself a testimony of faith in the alternative. He has added his beard to the illustrious greybeards before him whose visions would reform our moral bankruptcy. His devotion to this literary universe is perhaps most dramatically demonstrated in *The Novel Now*. Carol Dix makes the point when she observes: "As one critic of his survey of contemporary literature, *The Novel Now*, deduced from its bibliography, it seemed as if Burgess had been reading one contemporary novel a day, Sundays off, for the then six years of his active writing career. His general reading and his general and specific knowledge cannot pass unappraised." And our appraisal must be that it is impressive and indeed inspiring on all counts. *Beard's Roman Women* (1976) concludes on a humble, individual, and literarily uplifting note to the strains of Dryden's magnificent "Ode upon St. Cecilia's Day," with its promise that "music shall untune the sky." We leave Ronald Beard—his name the very culmination of the grey-bearded ghosts which haunt *One Hand Clapping*—"as happy as he had ever been in his life. Nothing left undone, and a whole night's drinking in front of him. The rain was teeming down now, and he'd actually got a taxi." Here is a literary man who has survived the hauntings of the past and the memory of his first wife long presumed dead, a writer who has transformed love, history, and the tortures of the battle into literary creativity, blessed by a cleansing baptismal rain. And in the end it is the taxi which has responded to human control, the machine which has listened to man's voice, the creation which has *stopped* at the creator's command.

ANTHONY BURGESS, the professional name of John Anthony Burgess Wilson, was born February 27, 1917, at Manchester, England, the son of Joseph and Elizabeth Burgess. After getting his B.A. at Manchester University in 1940, he married Llewella Jones in 1942 (she died in 1968). After the war, he served with the Ministry of Education and the British Colonial Service in Malaya and Borneo. After becoming ill in 1959, he devoted his full time to writing, producing an extraordinary series of novels in the early and mid 1960's. He remarried in 1968 (to Lilian Macellari), and has one son, Paolo. A list of his published works follows:

1. *Time for a tiger.* Heinemann, London, 1956, 214p, Cloth, Novel
2. *The enemy in the blanket.* Heinemann, London, 1958, 221p, Cloth, Novel
3. *English literature: a survey for students.* Longmans, Green, London, 1958, 340p, Cloth, Nonfiction
4. *Beds in the east.* Heinemann, London, 1959, 237p, Cloth, Novel
5. *The doctor is sick.* Heinemann, London, 1960, 260p, Cloth, Novel
6. *The right to an answer.* Heinemann, London, 1960, 255p, Cloth, Novel
7. *Devil of a state.* Heinemann, London, 1961, 282p, Cloth, Novel
8. *The worm and the ring.* Heinemann, London, 1961, 273p, Cloth, Novel
9. *One hand clapping.* Peter Davies, London, 1961, 205p, Cloth, Novel
10. *A clockwork orange.* Heinemann, London, 1962, 196p, Cloth, Novel
11. *The wanting seed.* Heinemann, London, 1962, 285p, Cloth, Novel
12. *Honey for the bears.* Heinemann, London, 1963, 255p, Cloth, Novel
13. *Inside Mr. Enderby.* Heinemann, London, 1963, 252p, Cloth, Novel [as Joseph Kell]
14. *The novel to-day.* Longmans, Green, London, 1963, 56p, Cloth, Nonf.
15. *Nothing like the sun.* Heinemann, London, 1964, 234p, Cloth, Novel
16. *The eve of Saint Venus.* Sidgwick & Jackson, London, 1964, 138p, Cloth, Novel
17. *The Malayan trilogy.* Pan, London, 1964, 512p, Paper, Coll. [Includes: *Time for a tiger, The enemy in the blanket,* and *Beds in the east*]
17A retitled: *The long day wanes.* W. W. Norton, New York, 1965, 512p, Cloth, Coll.
18. *Language made plain.* English Universities Press, London, 1964, 186p, Cloth, Nonfiction
19. *Here comes everybody.* Faber & Faber, London, 1965, 276p, Cloth, Nonfiction
19A retitled: *Re Joyce.* W. W. Norton, New York, 1965, 272p, Cloth, Nonf.
20. *A vision of battlements.* Sidgwick & Jackson, London, 1965, 265p, Cloth, Novel
21. *Tremor of intent.* Heinemann, London, 1966, 240p, Cloth, Novel

LITERATURE

Anthony Burgess

Anthony Burgess, the professional pseudonym of John Anthony Burgess Wilson, is one of the best-known writers of postwar Britain. He achieved early recognition in the 1950s with his Malayan novels, but only gained widespread acclaim with publication of *A Clockwork Orange* in 1962, later made into a hit movie by Stanley Kubrick. The world of *Clockwork* is a nightmare future England where teen-age gangs roam the streets after dark, raping and pillaging, where government ministers try to further their own careers by brainwashing criminals into giving up their lives of crime, making it physically impossible for them to even contemplate antisocial acts. A second dystopian novel, *The Wanting Seed,* looks further ahead, with even grimmer results: homosexuality is encouraged, infanticide is approved, and couples may have only one child without incurring official wrath. Richard Mathews discusses all of Burgess's work, from his first novel, *A Vision of Battlements,* to his most recent work of fiction, *Beard's Roman Women,* paying particular attention to the author's major novels of the 1960s, *The Eve of St. Venus, M/F, One Hand Clapping,* and *A Clockwork Orange.*

Dr. Richard Mathews has written three other books in the Borgo Press series, *Aldiss Unbound; The Science Fiction of Brian W. Aldiss, Lightning from a Clear Sky; Tolkien, the Trilogy, and the Silmarillion,* and *Worlds Beyond the World; the Fantastic Vision of William Morris.* He spends much of his free time producing a series of hand-made chapbooks on his Konglomerati Press, which he operates near his home in Gulfport, Florida.

The Borgo Press
P. O. Box 2845
San Bernardino, CA 92406

Cover Design
Judy Cloyd
ISBN 0-89370-227-7